PUBLIC –
PRIVATE –
PUBLIC

THE TRANSFORMATION IMPERATIVE

KEVIN J. KENNEDY

PUBLIC – PRIVATE – PUBLIC
The Transformation Imperative
By Kevin J. Kennedy

1. BUS015000 2. BUS077000 3. BUS104000
Print ISBN: 978-1-949642-17-9
Ebook ISBN: 978-1-949642-18-6
Audiobook ISBN: 978-1-949642-19-3

Cover design by Lewis Agrell

Printed in the United States of America

Authority Publishing
11230 Gold Express Dr. #310-413
Gold River, CA 95670
800-877-1097
www.AuthorityPublishing.com

DEDICATION

To the many customers, partners, and employees who engaged independently and collectively to transform an important provider of unique solutions.

To my wife, Barbara, for four decades of support, patience, and partnership.

TABLE OF CONTENTS

FOREWORDS

John Marren

Senior Managing Director of Temasek
Former Senior Partner and the Head of Technology Investments
of TPG Capital

As head of the technology investment group at TPG, I had a front-row seat as the decision was made to take Avaya private in 2007. TPG's belief in Avaya had been predicated on its strong business model and cash flow potential to support high-yield debt financing, but confidence in Avaya's future was sorely tested as the 2009 recession impacted every sector of the economy.

The effect of the Great Recession has been well documented—and its particular role in Avaya's transformation is clearly delineated within these pages. The bottom line is that a good asset became profoundly constrained by its own balance sheet. Legacy obligations and increasing high-yield debt service costs consumed the equity of the company.

Over a ten-year period, Avaya achieved an operational transformation that almost certainly could not have been executed in the public equity market. On the other hand, when the balance sheet is no longer sized for market conditions, a company often must go through a debt reorganization, which can be painful. The story here is that the excellence on operational metrics and a business model that improved by almost 200% enabled a successful debt reorganization and the re-emergence of the company as a public company.

This is a book about perseverance, operational focus, and pursuit of business model transformation. It is especially relevant to those interested in an operator's view of a large-scale technology transformation, in the nexus of private equity and technology, and in the dynamics of the customer care space. It is a story of how a team driven with intensity, operational command, self-awareness—along with a bias toward innovation and customer pull—completed the cycle from public to private to public, against enormous odds.

I was privileged to work alongside Kevin Kennedy through the full cycle of Avaya's transformation. He faithfully presents the story of what it's like to be in the driver's seat of such an intense and challenging journey, with insights and lessons along the way that are still relevant today.

Maggie Wilderotter

Chairman and CEO, Grand Reserve Inn
Former Chairman and CEO, Frontier Communications
Board of Directors of Lyft, Costco, HPE, Cadence Design Systems,
DocuSign

I first met Kevin Kennedy when we were board members at Quantum Corporation. Turns out Kevin and I had a few things in common: We had both grown up on the New Jersey shore, we were born in the same hospital, and we had been lured to California by the rising tide of technology. Since then, we have equally enjoyed the challenges and opportunities of businesses with unbridled growth—Kevin in data/internet and my journey in technology, mobility, and telecom. We both served as CEOs in the communications industry, leading assets through complete life cycles—including sustained transformation and consolidation stages.

As the CEO of Frontier Communications from 2004 to 2015, I was a key customer of Kevin's Avaya, so I had a vested interest in their ten-year transformation from a hardware to a software-and-services company, which culminated in December 2016. The scope of that transformation expanded dramatically in the wake of an unforeseen deep recession, which changed the assumptions behind the go-private business case. The most compelling aspects of Avaya's story are reflected in the extreme to which customer focus was indoctrinated and numerically advanced through operations and innovation; this—combined with the vast improvement of the business model to become a software-and-services company, which in turn drove a successful debt reorganization—ultimately enabled Avaya to go public again.

This book is not just the history of an important telecom asset. It explores a more prevalent, ongoing trend in technology, which is changing capital structures—from private to public to private to public. It does not preach how things should be; it speaks candidly about dealing with the world the way it is—including practical frameworks for navigating complexity, the perseverance required to reinvent runways in the wake of a deep recession, and much more. In short, it is a clear-minded and straightforward account of Avaya's remarkable journey, from the inside out.

As a customer and colleague, I valued Avaya's software expertise, and if ever a problem arose, Avaya's team responded quickly and skillfully to ensure the issue was resolved. Along the way, Kevin and I enjoyed a number of strategic exchanges; reading his book brought to life many of the operational challenges that I personally have wrestled with in my career, too.

As a business operator, I know very well that the leadership and dimensionality of skill required for a sustained transformation is very different from what it takes to drive companies that are all about growth. During the sustain-and-consolidate phases of a business transformation, leaders must be multi-dexterous in order to innovate a future while optimizing profits from the past. Leaders like Kevin must have commitment, tenacity, and grit to see it through; it *is* heavy lifting.

The value here is not merely in the details of achieving goals and a sustained transformation, but in the book's many insights to the life cycle of industries and companies that move in and out of the contemporary financial structures they live within. Avaya's path from public to private to public again is but one example of such a cycle, and it is illustrative and even compelling, given what was at stake. Allowing an AT&T legacy company to fail was simply not an option. I consider this book a must-read for seasoned and aspiring leaders of all industries, as disruption and technology are now part of the landscape. Enjoy Kevin's literary ride; I did!

Kenneth Kannappan

Former President and CEO of Plantronics

As CEO of Plantronics for eighteen years, I had a unique perspective on Avaya and the telecom industry: Plantronics' closest partner for more than fifty years was AT&T, its child Lucent, and its grandchild Avaya. As close as I was, I did not fully understand the complex challenges Avaya faced: Way behind in technology, rooted in an old business model, lagging in software and cloud, nowhere in services, needing to overcome cultural resistance, and buried under a heavy debt load during a massive recession and weak recovery. Quickly overcoming any of those challenges would have been remarkable. Overcoming them all was truly extraordinary.

This story isn't just valuable as history; it is instructive and inspirational. Kevin Kennedy had to create time to accomplish a company transformation during the Great Recession of 2008-09. At the time, some insiders maintained that little change was needed, but the industry's perspective was that Avaya's legacy business was dying and was likely to become a dinosaur as Unified Communications and SaaS models were cannibalizing its core business. In high tech the Darwinian model operates faster than in other industries: leaders are challenged to win the present war—survival of the fittest—while simultaneously evolving for change that is coming. Yet even if times are good and a little complacency hits our organizations as we prepare for the future, we rarely encounter so much cultural resistance—in this case, the unionized employee base of a former monopoly with more than a century behind it. The lessons on how to find the right leaders to quickly turn this around are enlightening.

With so many strategic, operational, and financial results to juggle at warp speed, it would be easy to feel overwhelmed. What comes through these pages is how Kevin maintained great clarity in the priorities, creating the calm and focus to enable his team to execute successfully. Honest communications—internally and with customers, even when things were tough—established credibility. Such trust allowed us to do things quickly as partners.

The book offers a few precious, personal nuggets about Kevin, but left out one of my favorites: When some on our respective teams were not making the desired progress on a joint project, Kevin reminded us all that the 102-story Empire State Building had been constructed in one year and forty-five days (long before computers or the advent of modern construction technology and equipment). It inspired everyone to stay focused and drive change more deliberately and creatively.

The value of this book is undeniable. At some point in their career, every leader needs to make changes to improve current business performance while preparing for future success. I wish I had read it decades ago.

PREFACE

As an engineering intern arriving at Bell Laboratories in Holmdel, New Jersey, in June 1976, I was understandably awestruck by the massive structure encased in shimmering glass, home to 5,000 engineers, scientists, and executives. I imagine my first impression akin to that of a software intern today, poised to enter the sweeping "spaceship" headquarters of Apple in Cupertino, California. But this was long before Apple, Google, or Microsoft, when the epicenter of the communications industry was New Jersey—home not only to AT&T, but to the innovation lab of Thomas Edison ("The Wizard of Menlo Park"), the Marconi Wireless Telegraph Company of America, and more.

"Ma Bell" was by then nearly 100 years old, one of the world's most highly capitalized companies, the seemingly invincible matriarch of virtually all telephone services in the United States and Canada. That she would be dismembered within a few short years seemed inconceivable; that I would have a front-row seat to the upheaval was just as unlikely.

My first assignment in AT&T's research and development division was to model the reliability of modems—devices that enabled computer data operations to communicate over voice networks. This product category was intriguing on many fronts. First, the digital era was nascent; the growth of all things digital was a certainty. In 1976, most people typed and punched computer cards and submitted batch programs into card readers. That said, the competition between the burgeoning computer world and the established voice-communications world was heating up at the same time AT&T was facing a major legal challenge because their products and services were seen as anti-competitive. By 1982, the arc of that challenge resulted in a historic decree to break up the Bell system; by 1984 divestiture was in motion. The telephony business would never be the same.

I spent seventeen years with the Bell System, including one pivotal year in Washington, DC, on a fellowship advising the House Committee on Science, Space and Technology on technical topics, the impact of export controls, industry regulation, and more. There I was introduced to political sparring and gamesmanship, as well as to governmental inefficiency and (sometimes) impropriety. After one year in the arena of influence and advising, I was eager to return to the world of making things and helping the Bell System advance their product portfolio.

In the wake of AT&T's divestiture between 1988 and 1993, I had the opportunity to work in the early stages of packet switching technology, followed by a later move to the emerging field of integrated voice response, i.e. systems that could recognize voice and initiate an outcome. In late 1993, Cisco offered me an opportunity to contribute to their development of internetworking solutions in the epic era of client server computing. Hence, our family followed the road west to California, along with others seeking to be part of the Silicon Valley "innovation rush."

The decade of the 1990s and early 2000s brought a reinvention of the telecom industry and enabled my immersion in executive roles at Cisco, Openwave mobile technology, JDS Uniphase optical technology, and later Avaya for enterprise communications.

This is not my story, per se. Yes, I lived it, but the real story is that of a technology company's transformation in a time of tremendous uncertainty. It is a tale of the past colliding with present and future—specifically, how a technology franchise had to continually reinvent itself as its capital structure changed and the market for its products and services matured.

For me personally, I never lost sight of the irony of leading the reorganization of a vestige of the legacy company where I had started as a young student more than thirty years before. What I learned during my CEO tenure at Avaya—a large company in need of transformation, with a private-equity capital structure—may be instructive for any CEO, board member, MBA student, corporate manager, or other student of the business landscape.

INTRODUCTION

To help put Avaya's story in perspective, it should be noted that in the early to mid-1970s, established communications platforms were beginning to absorb technologies such as semiconductors for digital efficiency, and microprocessors and software for programmability. Microsoft and Apple were founded in 1975 and 1976, respectively, as part of a world that would commoditize computing. Cisco launched in 1984 to meet the necessity and value of exchanging data between disparate computing platforms and applications. Amazon and Google came along in the mid- to late-1990s as the internet evolved to crystallize the dynamic of the world wide web. My arrival at AT&T coincided with the beginning of the destabilization of the communications industry and the emergence of today's technology titans.

On the competitive front of the Bell System's world at the time, two key product categories were the modem and the private branch exchange (PBX). One of these would have a runway of less than twenty years as a stand-alone company; the other is still reinventing itself forty-five years later. The saga of the modem is best observed by the trajectory of Hayes Microcomputer Inc., the market share leader and innovator (reaching over 50% market share), which released its first product in 1977. The company liquidated in 1999 as broadband communications disrupted the dial-up interconnection market. In contrast, the arc of the PBX continues to this day, and this book explores a critical period in the reinvention of a specific company, Avaya, as well as the broader communications industry. Two product categories born in the same decade, albeit one with half the longevity of the other, underscores the risk in innovation.

In the world of technology, a "runway" is the amount of time a startup needs to get up to speed before it launches into the next stage—or it crashes. Runway is calculated by dividing a business's current cash position by its monthly burn rate. Even well-established organizations have to construct their own runways to enable taking off and landing, sometimes repeatedly, in the face of increasingly rapid changes in technology, the marketplace, and the world: Change or die.

The consent decree in January 1982 and subsequent divestiture of the Bell System in 1984 became a seminal transition to separate runways for new and independent assets. Beyond the long distance and regional operating companies, new company runways were constructed, one of which was for the spinout of AT&T Technologies. That lasted ten years. In 1995, Lucent Technologies was spun off with its own runway. A mere five years later, Avaya went public as a spin-off from Lucent.

In 2007, Avaya was taken private and removed from the public equity market upon being acquired by Silver Lake Partners and Texas Pacific Group. These firms believed that as a private company Avaya would achieve significant operational improvements and move to a new business model. The goal was to increase the value of Avaya and allow it to reemerge as a public company.

Shortly after going private, the headwinds of the Great Recession and a substantially debt-based capital structure drove the need for a new operational runway. After the acquisition of Nortel Enterprise Solutions in 2010, Avaya completely changed its productivity and business model. However, the last elements of transforming the company required a reorganization of debt levels computed and galvanized before the Great Recession. The company chose to file for Chapter 11 debt reorganization in January 2017 and emerged back on the New York Stock Exchange in December 2017 with a more rational capital structure.

What follows is a powerful case study that charts the path of Avaya's transformation from the historical perspective that led to the company's privatization—as seen from the perspective of a CEO who jumped on board just before a major economic recession staggered the US and world economies—to the mission-driven focus on the business model, innovation, services, and customers, which enables any business to survive the forces of change.

Avaya's drive to transformation is noteworthy on several fronts: the scale of the company, the number of transitions required, the change in the business model, and the level of customer loyalty necessary for survival. Equally significant is that the process was rooted in a number of *pioneering* initiatives: the concept of customer success, the drive toward a cloud-first agenda, the pivot to services and subscriptions, and the embrace of new technologies (e.g., virtualization and containerization) that would become standard methods and tools in IT. Also unusual was the level of excellence achieved to reach record business-model metrics. The business model became the key to Avaya's survival—against the odds.

As we look across industries in 2018 and beyond, it is clear that digital transformation will continue disrupting every industry, impacting the need for companies to transform themselves to extend their runways in order to survive. Furthermore, private equity ownership in concert with the prevalence of debt on corporate balance sheets shows no sign of throttling. Although Avaya's story examines the strategies, tools, and perspectives brought to bear on a unique situation, it is a case study with wider applicability in the larger mosaic of increasingly rapid and sometimes bewildering change.

~ 1 ~

STORM CLOUDS ON THE HORIZON

As I arrived in January 2009 at Avaya's headquarters in Basking Ridge, New Jersey, to begin my role as Avaya's CEO—its fourth in three years—I noticed a woman approaching who was bundled up against the cold, blustery day. I took out my new badge to open the door for her. She entered the lobby. Then suddenly she turned back toward me and demanded, "How *dare* you open the door for me?"

I was stunned at the level of hostility in response to a simple act of courtesy. Was she just having a bad day, or was more going on? Had Avaya's recent instability generated such fear and distrust among its employees? And if a disgruntled worker could treat a fellow employee this way, what might it say about how other Avaya workers represent the company to customers and other stakeholders? Whatever the answers to these questions might be, it was an unsettling start to my new journey.

I took the elevator up to the third floor, entered my office, and spoke briefly with my new assistant. After a few minutes, I decided to discuss the incident with Pamela Craven, Avaya's Chief Administrative Officer and General Counsel. Pam—bright, thoughtful, and reflective—had been part of the company's initial management team when it was spun out from Lucent Technologies in 2000. If anyone could explain what had happened just now, it might be Pam.

I described the woman's outburst. Pam said she could not be certain, but she remarked that for many years Lucent Technologies had placed employees on a work-reduction list by counting the days they did not come to work. Since I'd used my badge for both of us to enter, Pam suggested the woman may have thought I was pre-empting her attendance count, thereby putting her job at risk. I found this incomprehensible. But if it *was* true, I wondered what other well-established cultural constraints would need to be overcome in the process of transforming Avaya.

That incident became emblematic of my central question in those early days: How much would the drag of the past inhibit the chances for Avaya's future? To be more specific: In spite of the firm's legacy of innovation and industry dominance, operationally it was an anachronism—a hardware business model, operated and managed by too many entitled individuals. It was a flawed inheritance. I went home that day filled with great uncertainty; among other things, to what extent would the prevailing, entrenched emotions and beliefs undermine the reason and logic that I knew was badly needed? And would Avaya's recent history merely *compound* everyone's natural fear of the unknown?

> *How much would the drag of the past inhibit Avaya's future?*

Aside from that inauspicious opening salvo, other cautionary signs contrasted with my experience of twenty years in Silicon Valley. There, I was accustomed to managers and individual contributors mingling freely; blue jeans and open shirts were common; wealth and status were almost impossible to discern by appearance alone.

Not so at Avaya, where suits and ties were *de rigueur,* and my new C-suite was four times larger than my office at JDS Uniphase in California.

My concerns about Avaya's culture and the challenges ahead were further complicated during my first series of meetings with top executives, five of whom informed me they were leaving.

A NEW MISSION

I was well aware that Avaya had to transform from an historic focus on telecommunications hardware to a software and services company in line with the realities of the telecommunications marketplace where rapid innovation is the norm. It was clear that such innovation would have to be internally driven and supported by monies saved by eliminating waste and greatly increasing efficiency.

There was a belief among the board, leadership team, and analysts' coverage that the company was overly complex, and that complexity kills companies. Avaya would have to simplify organizationally by improving operations, eliminating silos, automating out waste, and divesting assets that would otherwise suffocate the chances for improvement.

In my mind and that of the board, the timetable for such dramatic change was five years or less. But it took much longer. The unexpected Great Recession of 2008-09 was a significant setback, and changing the cultural norms proved to be equally challenging.

A RICH HERITAGE – PROS AND CONS

As noted in the Introduction, Avaya's roots stretch back more than 140 years to the first attempts to develop the telephone by two pioneering inventors, one still famous and the other largely forgotten.

In 1876, Alexander Graham Bell was in Boston experimenting with "harmonic telegraphy." Bell knew that another inventor, Elisha

Gray in Cleveland, was working on a similar device at the same time, and he felt enormous pressure to complete his design first. On February 14, 1876, Gray's lawyer submitted a *patent caveat* to the US Patent Office in Washington, DC. However, earlier that day Bell's lawyer had submitted *his* client's patent application based on technology similar to Gray's "water transmitter." Under circumstances that would be debated for years, the patent was granted to Bell on March 7, 1876.

Three days later, the "Eureka" moment came. On the evening of March 10, Bell was near a transmitter and Thomas Watson, his assistant, was in another room close to the receiver. According to legend (disputed by some sources), Bell, renowned for his clumsiness, spilled a vial of battery acid and instinctively shouted into the transmitter, "Mr. Watson—come here—I want to see you." Watson heard Bell's cry and raced over. Once together, the two men realized they had finally created the world's first functioning voice-transmission device. Within a year, 230 Bostonians had bought telephones, which led to the establishment of the Bell Telephone Company in 1877. Eight years later, AT&T was formed to create a national long-distance network.

By 1940, AT&T, now headquartered in New York, was the largest corporation in the world, effectively owning every aspect of telephone service in the United States and Canada, from local and long-distance service to the telephones themselves. At that time, it had four major divisions:

- AT&T - interconnected local exchanges and long-distance calling services
- Western Electric - Bell's equipment manufacturing arm
- Bell Labs - research and development
- Bell Operating Companies - providers of local exchange telephone services

The two jewels of this system were Western Electric and Bell Labs.

Bell Labs engaged in a vast range of basic and applied research as part of its mission to develop telecommunications equipment and systems. It became one of the greatest scientific organizations in the world—producing seven Nobel Prize winners and some of the most important technological advances of the twentieth century, such as research on semiconductors that led to the invention of the transistor, and the discovery of background microwave radiation that helped substantiate the "Big Bang" theory of the origin of the universe.

Western Electric manufactured all the telephones in areas where AT&T subsidiaries provided local service, all components of the public switched telephone network (PSTN), and all devices connected to the network.

One of the products that emerged from AT&T in the 1970s and ultimately became the core of Avaya was called the private branch exchange (more commonly known as PBX). Automating the previously manually operated switchboards in companies or institutions, the PBX provided a concentrated connection to the switched telephone network, eliminated the need for switchboards and operators, and offered cost-effective business telephony services. Other critical functions that evolved as the PBX spread were Contact Center software (e.g., for dialing 911 or toll-free assistance) and integrated voice response for self-service.

Despite such technological advances as the PBX, the long reign of AT&T as America's monopolistic provider of telephone service and telephone equipment began to unravel when the US Department of Justice in 1974 launched an antitrust case that eventually forced the company to divest its ownership of Western Electric and other assets.

In 1984, a newly formed company, AT&T Technologies, Inc., assumed the corporate charter of Western Electric, which was split into several divisions, each focusing on a particular type of customer, e.g., AT&T Technology Systems, and AT&T Network Systems. Western Electric officially came to an end in 1995 when AT&T changed the name of AT&T Technologies to Lucent Technologies in preparation for its spinoff. Many employees of Bell Labs became part of Lucent, which became independent in 1996.

On January 6, 2000, Lucent made the first of a string of announcements that it had missed its quarterly estimates, reporting flat revenues and a big drop in profits. Its stock plunged 28%, shaving $64B off the company's market capitalization. In April 2000, Lucent sold its Consumer Products unit to VTech and Consumer Phone Services. And in October 2000, Lucent spun off its Business Systems arm into what became Avaya. Some years later, Lucent merged with Alcatel of France.

The post-spinout period was an opportunity for Avaya; its new capital structure enabled acquisitions but also brought the struggle of being a public company with daily stock price fluctuations. In the words of one former long-time, mid-level manager at Avaya, "During the period from 2000 to 2007, Avaya employees rode a rollercoaster!" They watched a $17 stock price drop to $1, they navigated the arrival and departure of several CEOs, and they endured numerous headcount reductions—all of which led to survival-oriented entrenchment.

This, then, is Avaya's pedigree: groundbreaking innovation, determined and brilliant individuals, and constant transformation in response to altered market conditions. At the same time, Avaya inherited a legacy of enormous operational inertia, partly the result of AT&T's century-long monopoly: attitudes of personal entitlement, inflexible processes to achieve scale without taking risk, and a sense of survival that subjugated urgency in spite of changes in the marketplace.

Two quotes stand out concerning this inheritance. A Western Electric general manager once told me: "If it is not the same, it is different; and if it is different, I am not doing it." Charlie Giancarlo, a former Silverlake operating partner and interim Avaya CEO before me, said: "Avaya is a museum of anachronistic business practices proven not to work from *before* 1980."

The challenges confronting the Avaya leadership team in 2009—of a legacy company with an antiquated, change-resistant culture, non-competitive business practices, and a complex corporate structure—were well known. What wasn't so clear was the full impact of the Great Recession and other factors soon to be revealed.

~ 2 ~

GETTING UNDERWAY

As the new CEO of Avaya, my mission unknowingly began at a moment when America and much of the world was close to a potential economic collapse.

What became known as the Great Recession actually began in late 2007 due to the crisis with subprime mortgages and collateralized debt obligations. It escalated in 2008 with astonishing speed, metastasizing and reaching broader segments of the world economy. At one point, almost the entire banking system froze. Lending institutions hoarded cash to write-down bad mortgages and to create a hedge against bank runs. Hoarding led to an increase in interest rates which, in turn, raised the cost of loans. The result was a cash shortage for many businesses, including General Motors and Chrysler, which teetered on the edge of insolvency. By June of 2009, Gross Domestic Product (GDP) growth had shrunk by 8%.

In response, the Federal Reserve dropped its interest rate to near zero and poured billions into short-term loans to banks and money market funds to shore up the financial system. Despite these attempts, major institutions failed: the investment bank Bear Stearns was bought by J.P. Morgan Chase; the Treasury Department seized mortgage companies Fannie Mae and Freddie Mac and converted them back into government agencies; then in September Lehman Brothers collapsed. Several days later the Fed became the primary shareholder of the insurance giant AIG, spending $85B initially and later an additional $150B.

By year's end, the Dow was down 34%, closing at 8,816.62. Other indices were worse—the S&P 500 ended at 907.22, a 38% decline. The Dow fell 25% in October alone from 10,831 on October 1 to 8,175 on October 27. It reached its low of 7,552 on November 20, a 46% drop from its October 2007 high of 14,164.

In retrospect, January 2009 was a dubious time to begin as the new head of a major corporation. The tone for my mission may have been foretold one month earlier when I moved from California to Avaya's company headquarters in Basking Ridge, New Jersey. The weather had been as stormy and unprecedented as the economy, one of the wettest in 114 years of record keeping. Heavy rains, ice, and winds on the 12th of December had snapped trees and power lines throughout the region and had caused widespread highway flooding. Seven days later, a powerful storm dumped ten inches of snow on the area.

In the last week of December and before reporting to work, I had scanned the most recent quarter's results and specifically the December orders. Order rates were down roughly 30% in one quarter. (Normal seasonal drop would be in the 3-4% range.) The cause was the plummeting GDP. Companies weren't spending on anything, including telecommunications. Historically there is a particularly strong correlation between GDP and unified communications orders—rising GDP drives employment and the need for communications gear; falling GDP, fewer orders. If this trend continued unabated, Avaya would be in serious trouble.

Drastic times demand immediate action. As one might expect, a phone call to Avaya's CFO was my first task. I asked him if the company had a plan for dealing with the bookings problem. It did not.

Part of the phlegmatic response could be attributed to the nature of the business. It was not unusual for 60% of the orders to be received in the last month of the year, with a majority in the final week. There existed historic grounds for optimism or at least not overreacting. But this year was anything but usual.

CREATING A SHARED VISION

Given the immediate crisis, the lack of a plan, and a growing realization that Avaya would need years to recover, I believed the situation called for a major structural change. The term "turnaround" does not apply here; put simply, Avaya needed a *transformation*. It is very important to be clear on the difference: A turnaround can happen when a company has lost its way and executed poorly but still needs to compete in the same product market/space. A transformation is needed when a company must fundamentally alter its financial, operational, and strategic trajectory, which is a far more difficult and lengthy process. A turnaround calls for improved focus, optimizations, and realignment for success over a period of quarters; transformation demands disassembly of the past and reinvention of the future, with outcomes occurring over years.

> *Drastic times demand immediate action.*

My first decision was to hire a Chief Restructuring Officer (CRO) to work closely with me to devise a plan to drive fundamental change. We needed a radical plan for Avaya to weather the unknown magnitude and duration of this economic crisis.

Of all the executives that I interviewed when I first arrived, Jim Chirico stood out as best able to fill the role of CRO. He was already running operations and managing Avaya's supply chain. Jim had joined the company in January 2008, so he was not someone who had been part of Avaya's culture for a long time (a big plus in my mind). In addition, he was very experienced at managing a large workforce. He had come from Seagate Technology, an American data storage company that dominates the hard disk drive market. At Seagate, he had been Executive Vice President for Global Operations, Development, and Manufacturing, leading a team of more than 50,000 employees in fourteen facilities worldwide, and successfully driving a step-function change in the operational effectiveness of the organization. Prior to Seagate, Jim had been at IBM for eighteen years. He proved to be the ideal candidate for our mission.

By New Year's Eve, I had sent an email to the board to make sure they were fully aware of the perilous state of things; the company's trend in orders and the impact of the recession called for an immediate response to avoid being cash flow negative for the year. We needed a strategy— more accurately, broad and decisive intervention—to meet this crisis, and fast.

On the first business day of the new year, two operational advisors, sent by the board, arrived at Avaya to welcome me and offer their help. Their intention was to assist me in building value in the company and to provide guidance in the company's transformation. They expressed a concern of the board—don't "break the company." Over time they provided me with a "back channel" to the board regarding the developments on the ground and they served as a sounding board for advancing ideas.

Fairly quickly, we put together a plan that included an evolving set of initiatives including but not limited to:

1. Sizing the company for a new economy, including changes to headcount, structure, redundancies, footprint, etc. Initially, we concentrated on non-business areas.
2. Reducing expenses with temporary measures such as furloughs—top executives taking three weeks off and other employees two weeks.

3. Temporarily cancelling variable compensation (i.e., bonuses) for all employees.
4. Reducing the amount of external spending on consultants, suppliers, et al.
5. Eliminating entitlements, such as Avaya's fleet of private planes and their hangars, as well as suspending more general entitlements such as a 401k matching program during the recession.
6. Eliminating waste and redundancy.
7. Automating and reducing touch-based functions.

In addition, from a talent perspective, I decided to have all employees rated on a performance scale. The rating consisted both of numbers and soft measures of attitude. As quickly as possible, we wanted to break the culture of entitlement that was endemic to Avaya. This process would help us retain the employees who were performing at a high level and eliminate those who were not. Equally important, if and when the recession ebbed and business conditions improved, clarity on best performers would help guide us in how to prioritize incentive pay.

Of course, the above actions were difficult, were required for survival, and were potentially threatening to the status quo. These actions entailed increased severance and reorganizational costs, but *not* taking these actions would have been much worse for all concerned, in the near term.

We initiated a plan to break down company silos. For example, departments such as sales, marketing, research and development, et al. rarely communicated with one another. We also began to eliminate the multiple approval levels needed for projects to go forward. At that time, in some situations, up to seventeen levels of approval were needed! Overall, we reduced approval steps to a few or several in most cases.

At the end of the first couple of weeks, we discussed our plan in detail with the board. We made the case that Avaya would run out of money before the end of 2009 if we continued with business as usual. The board listened intently and responded with cautious support to proceed.

In implementing the plan, I knew that the answers to four primary questions held the keys to our success:

(1) **How bad was the recession going to be?** How deep will the fall be, how long will it last, what will economic conditions be when the world emerges from it? We would have to stay nimble and react as quickly as possible to the twists and turns in the economy and the decisions being made by the Federal Reserve, the White House, and Congress.

(2) **How should we manage the restructuring of Avaya?** In my mind, it was going to take a long time. This would prove to be the most substantial challenge. We will say much more about the "how" in subsequent chapters.

(3) **How long will it take to develop a more optimized leadership team?** Where would we find new executives not held back by a culture steeped in the past? We knew such executives existed. They were what we came to call ambidextrous leaders—courageous but without excessive ego—leaders who could disassemble the past while inventing the future. But we also knew such leaders were uncommon and hard to find. We had to start by developing criteria to help identify them.

(4) **What new initiatives and metrics would lead Avaya back to being first-class?** From prior transformation work, I had a good sense of what these would be. With the help of others, the executive team aligned and became convinced these initiatives and metrics could be implemented at Avaya.

Overall, our vision was to tear down and rebuild Avaya's product offer from static legacy communications to programmable and software-defined communications. Beginning such a transformation during a deep recession ensured that we would encounter significant "headwinds" to thwart progress. Understanding the headwinds (the subject of the next chapter) is key to fully understanding the "how" of Avaya's transformation and appreciating the extent to which the odds were stacked against success.

~ 3 ~

HEADWINDS

Well before the economic collapse of 2008-09, leaders who had survived the bursting of the telecom bubble in 2001-02 came away with important lessons that are worth noting here. In the wake of a recession or other disruption to any industry:

- The mix of product revenues post-downturn will vary dramatically from pre-downturn, favoring new-generation products post-downturn. Prior to the optics industry reset in 2001, for example, long-haul optics represented the volume of business; following the 2001 bubble exhaust, metropolitan access networks drove growth in new categories of optics.
- It is not uncommon to have dramatic average selling price compression, sometimes by an order of magnitude or more.
- Downturns bring protracted periods of inventory burn-off or asset sweating, and each customer begins to turn on the purchasing spigot at a different time, case by case. Do not expect a "bounce" back.

- There may be fewer customers as they exit businesses or go out of business themselves.
- There may be new competitors (startups or large companies that attack through adjacencies).
- Customers will routinely focus on terms, conditions, and savings on recurring costs. In short, procurement organizations focus on near-term purchasing details to lower run-rate expense.
- Customers will right-size as their employee ranks are reduced, thereby placing downward top-line pressure on recurring revenues that are per-employee based.

With those lessons in mind, as the realities of the Great Recession intersected with the implications of transformation, Avaya was facing eleven major headwinds—all direct threats to top-line revenues, notwithstanding non-company specific items such as foreign exchange ebbs and flows. These headwinds can best be summarized in four categories:

A. RECESSION-DRIVEN HEADWINDS

1. Customer dislocation – Fewer customers post-recession: As a consequence of the 2008-09 recession, a number of companies went out of business, others merged, and some cut spending dramatically. Banking and pharmaceutical mergers and reductions in force reduced revenue in these two highly concentrated sectors. Defense spending pullback also adversely impacted Avaya revenues.
2. Asset sweating – Clients decided to let their hardware and software age and did not upgrade to the most recent releases.
3. Recurring revenues targeted – Customers sought deep discounts as part of survival on service categories such as maintenance and support. In many cases, the ultimatum

was to give the discount or be replaced by a competitor supplier. Other unfavorable contract terms were added.

B. CUSTOMER-DRIVEN HEADWINDS

1. Transition from historical models to new models: In Avaya's case, the embrace of mobile phones and reduction of the ratio of fixed desk phones. Since fixed phones represented roughly 30% of the business, a change in phone volumes would deliver notable impacts to yearly revenues.
2. One-time cap-ex models lose favor to operating expense and managed services—new consumption models, e.g. subscription (pay as you go) and cloud-based (SaaS) services. In short: Large, one-time revenue recognition was now distributed over years.
3. Deferred spending: Waiting for the promise of next-generation products, including omni-channel and digital transformation.

C. INDUSTRY-DRIVEN / COMPETITIVE STRUCTURE HEADWINDS

1. In the Unified Communications space, as new competitors emerged from adjacencies, specifically Cisco and Microsoft, they used profit sanctuary cross-subsidies to establish beach-heads at very low rates, commoditizing the average selling prices in the category.
2. The industry shift from hardware to software eliminated vendor-supplied services, which lowered new revenues (since hardware was no longer provided) although it drove up gross margins for what was transacted.

D. Avaya-Specific Headwinds

1. Known divestitures, ten in total, more than half of which impacted the top line, but all made the bottom line improve.
2. Dis-synergies from the merged Avaya/Nortel product categories created an ongoing ebb. These dis-synergies included the elimination of duplicate, legacy, or increasingly stale products and services.
3. Shifting paths to market—especially an increase in sales through its channel partners, from direct to indirect. More services were provided by partners so more discounting took place, resulting in lower revenues.

An estimation of the collective quantification of downward revenue pressure can be efficiently framed by assessing the adverse impacts of the following subsets:

1. M&A divestitures over nine years resulted in a decline of more than $500M in revenue, with a loss of absolute EBITDA of less than $100M. The two largest contributors here were the divestiture of the networking business and the PEC, a services business for US government-cleared talent.
2. Nortel revenue dis-synergies dropped non-uniformly over time, but with a mean level in the range of $100M per year.
3. The advent of mobile phones being used in lieu of fixed handsets reduced the ratio of handsets per line from 2 to 1, so we began to observe handset volumes drop in half, cutting top line revenues by hundreds of millions per year.
4. Reduced recurring revenues due to customers merging or going out of business impacted revenues by $10M-$60M per quarter.

Suffice to say that Avaya's headwinds had the potential to reduce the run rate of revenues in excess of $1.5B to $2.0B per year.

OVERCOMING THE HEADWINDS IN REVENUE

With this amount of downward pressure in the pipeline and given that we did not know the timing of how these forces would collide, it was essential that Avaya come up with a business model improvement plan that did not assume revenue optimism. Furthermore, with 75%-80% of revenues delivered through a myriad of channel partners, new revenue adoption would occur slowly, so replacement revenue absent big acquisitions was unlikely.

It was necessary to take management forecasts in any given year with caution. Predictability was challenging at best.

Salesforce input in concert with industry forecasts were plotted. Then, an organic revenue decline was also plotted for the median of the past eight years. Next, a worst-case envelope was assessed. It was also known that not all adverse forces would have the same rate of impact on all geographies at the same time. So, keeping a healthy international business was important, as was thoughtful judgment about rates of impact of the above headwinds.

Headwinds could reduce the run rate of revenues more than $1.5 to $2.0B per year.

The point here is that given the lack of revenue predictability, the cost basis and transformation programs were assembled in case of outcomes on the conservative side of the range, such that the business model and net EBITDA would improve somewhat independent of top-line predictability. With this understanding, it was possible to focus transformation initiatives around revenue growth and predictability vs. the nature of the cost structure (i.e., fixed vs. variable).

In the chart below, the vertical axis is bound by:

a) at the top, high growth and high predictability
b) at the bottom, decline and low predictability

The X axis is bounded by fixed costs, and variable costs.

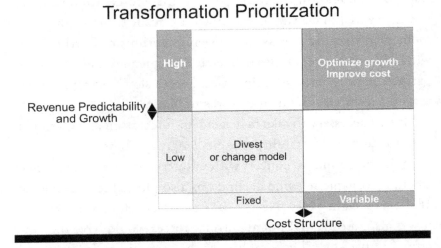

Figure 1: Transformation Prioritization

Where there was a high fixed cost base and low revenue predictability with declines, this would be a crucial focus area for restructuring toward a new model. The movement to self-service and the web and customer support became an example of this. Where the cost basis was largely variable and there existed growth and predictability for revenues, optimizing the variable cost further became important in concert with accelerating revenue further. In this case, when variable costs improved and revenue grew, both top and bottom lines improved predictably. The Contact Center application area was one such example.

With the transitions above and a perspective on how to ensure EBITDA growth independent of top-line trajectories in any period, it was crucial to look at new metrics of demand since one-time revenues were being transformed into recurring payments over perhaps twelve to twenty quarters. This transition was captured by monitoring a metric called Total Demand Under Contract, which subsumed one-time revenues, recurring maintenance, long-term contracts booked and recognizable, and so forth. In short, if Total Demand Under Contract was stable, new recurring revenue streams would eventually lift recognized quarterly revenues.

By the end of 2016, the company evidenced a flat trend in Total Demand Under Contract, while the Contact Center specifically showed growth in one-time, recurring, *and* Total Demand Under Contract. The point here is that the application side of the business with the healthiest industry structure was pulling the company to growth despite the many headwinds.

With the process described for navigating many top-line unknowns, a discussion on the framework of the transformation is possible (see next chapter). It is worth noting that any management team is expected at most to handle one to three headwinds at a time; five would require a Herculean effort on any sustained basis. That the Avaya board and company leaders simultaneously managed eleven different headwinds speaks volumes about their vision and courage.

~ 4 ~

THE TRANSFORMATION
IMPERATIVE

E ven in the face of significant headwinds, Avaya's leadership team held firm to eight core beliefs that informed their strategy and guided decision making:

- **Simplification is crucial; complexity destroys.** This principle led us to ten divestitures over nine years, the outsourcing of non-core activities, and a focus on lowering costs. We reduced silos, disassembled and reinvented processes, and introduced new systems.
- **Avaya needs to shrink before it can grow.** Growth in revenue required a new and sustainable business model—from high revenue/lower margin hardware to lower revenue/ higher margin software.
- **Innovation is crucial to a private-equity based company.** Without a public-equity market float, Avaya did not have the firepower to buy technology at levels greater than its competitors. Innovation—especially organically sourced— was essential.

- **Extended transformation requires a focus on the customer.** In a best-outcome scenario, an increase in Net Promoter Score (NPS) success would be a differentiator; even if outcomes fell short, we still expected the effort to improve customer loyalty and increase revenue.

- **Innovation is essential to NPS leadership.** We believed that delivering innovation not available elsewhere to customers was key to improving the Net Promoter Score, but this was hard to justify or quantify in advance.

- **Operational metric attainment could surpass benchmarks.** Most benchmarks are derived as an average or median of a group, even an assembly of data points in the top quartile. We believed that once the company built a culture and system around automating, eliminating waste, and improving quality with cycle time, the company could overachieve industry group norms in the depth and breadth of its metrics.

- **Internal resistance to change should not be underestimated.** Employee desire for long-term survival can produce an inert culture. Resistance at Avaya came from many directions, and in many forms, so we had to be clear on what had to change, and how.

- **Systems require compliance on a daily basis.** Sustainable change requires new systems and the elimination of inconsistent execution as people change. Said another way: Patching issues with people brought temporary change but regression later. True systemic change brings reportable precision in outcomes and can help transform a culture from an old to a new state.

By the middle of 2009, the urgency of Avaya's transformation imperative was amplified as the Great Recession continued to eviscerate assumptions about the economy and market that framed the capital structure in privatization. In particular, three core assumptions were rendered irrelevant by the macroeconomics post-2008, and most especially impacted cash flow projections over time:

1. Recession vs. no recession – Impacted assumptions on cash, revenue growth or decline, etc. A deeper recession also drove restructuring, which consumes cash.

2. Long-term GDP growth – Impacted market and company growth rates which in turn affected projections on cash flow. Lower or negative growth inhibited cash flow and limited the company in delevering.

3. Interest rates – Sustained lower interest rates drove higher pension payments. While possibly counterintuitive, the debt service required for underfunded corporate pension plans depends on two elements: actuarial and discount rates. Longer life expectancies and lower interest rates work in concert to increase debt service obligations. (See Robert Pozner, "The Underfunding of Corporate Pension Plans.")

Despite this, Avaya aligned around a set of initiatives for both near-term survival and long-term advancement. A primary focus was how to handle a looming crisis—Avaya was capitalized with substantial debt and other obligations (e.g., pensions) while also dealing with a strong revenue contraction and a conversion from revenue to EBITDA of between 10% and 15% of revenue. The runway for paying our continued debt obligations could shorten dramatically if the macroeconomic environment worsened or stayed negative for long.

> *The Great Recession eviscerated assumptions about the economy and market that framed the capital structure of privatization.*

No matter what, business model expansion—i.e., the conversion of EBITDA as a percent of revenue—needed to expand to ensure an ongoing runway.

Nortel Casts a Shadow

Our concerns regarding the runway were reinforced when a "cousin" of Avaya's in the telecom space, Nortel Enterprise Solutions, filed for Chapter 11 protection on January 14, 2009.

Nortel, like Avaya, was a legacy voice company that had begun as Northern Electric, a 1960s-era pioneer in the use of fiber optic cable and digital switching systems; they supplied equipment for Bell Telephone Company of Canada. In 1998, the company's name was changed to Nortel Networks to denote its ability to provide complete solutions for multi-protocol, multi-service, global networking over the internet and other communications networks.

In 2000, Bell Canada Enterprise spun out Nortel—the same year Lucent spun out Avaya—creating two "orphans" in the public market. At its apex, Nortel had accounted for more than a third of the total valuation of all companies listed on the Toronto Stock Exchange (TSX). They employed 94,500 worldwide, 25,900 of whom were in Canada. Between September 2000 and August 2002, Nortel's market capitalization fell from $398B to less than $5B; their stock price plunged from $124 to $0.47 a share.

Nortel underwent a dramatic restructuring, laying off two-thirds of its workforce and writing-down nearly $16B in 2001 alone. This generated some initial success, but a series of accounting scandals hurt the company.

After announcing its decision to file Chapter 11 in 2009, Nortel's share price fell more than 79% on the Toronto Stock Exchange. At that time, Nortel Enterprise Solutions' economic yield on Avaya equivalent business was roughly 4% EBITDA/revenue; hence, its operating income and cash flow were negative.

Initially Nortel had hoped to emerge from Chapter 11 protection, but circumstances worked against them: The worsening recession and the stock market decline deterred potential companies from bidding for its assets, and many of Nortel's major customers reconsidered their relationships with the restructuring company. By June 2009, Nortel announced that it would seek buyers for all of its business units.

Avaya won an auction for Nortel Enterprise Solutions' business, including Nortel's stake in Nortel Government Solutions and DiamondWare, for $900M. Although this move increased Avaya's debt burden in the short-term, the long-term strategy was to expand its PBX business where market overlap was minimal. (At the time, most of those familiar with the situation recognized the irony, given Nortel's unsuccessful move to buy Avaya in 2006-07, prior to the private equity buyout.)

THREE STRATEGIC LEVERS

Avaya's purchase of Nortel Enterprise Solutions underscored three strategic levers essential to a sustainable and positive new capital structure. All three levers depended on how well we could manage the level of our debt, pension, and restructuring obligations, as well as the extent and speed of operational transformation.

The levers were:

1. **Improve the operational performance** of the core Avaya asset—i.e., significantly improve EBITDA as a percent of revenue and drive the company toward software and services.
2. **Increase the size of the company**—i.e., expand the perimeter and optimize the operational performance of this incremental asset expansion.
3. **Plan and be positioned for the return of pre-recession conditions** favorable for more normal GDP growth, interest

rates, and restructuring levels. (Higher interest rates would reduce pension contribution requirements to earlier levels.) In short: Extend the runway of debt service to enable macro conditions to drive balance sheet improvement and growth.

At the heart of the efficacy of the three levers was a call to arms around operational transformation: The more productive the yield from revenue to EBITDA, the more the company would have a favorable runway. The company proceeded to execute on the three levers.

The first results of the impact of the Nortel acquisition were reported in 2010. Revenues grew quarter over quarter by almost $220M with product revenues larger than services revenues—i.e., roughly 55% in a company that had been dominated by services revenues for some time.

The combined EBITDA as a percentage of revenue was just north of 11%, however. Debt was increased and the net debt/ EBITDA ratio moved from 5.3 to 6.1. If other debt-like obligations were considered in this ratio, the net effective debt/EBITDA was moving well in excess of 7, a threshold generally viewed to be an uncomfortable level of risk. Therefore, improving EBITDA in absolute terms and EBITDA/revenue yield was crucial.

Next, we began a systematic process to drive transformation with what we called the CLIMB model (the subject of the next chapter). The mandate for and the execution of improved transformation metrics far exceeded any pre-going private assumptions. For example, assumptions in the privatization business model were that Avaya would achieve a sustainable EBITDA/ revenue of 22%. Instead, by the end of F2016, Avaya delivered a

> *Transformation demands disassembly of the past and reinvention of the future.*

near-record $940M of EBITDA with a yield of 25.4% for the year and 29% for fiscal Q4 of 2016, both all-time highs. By this time, the mix of business had transformed to more than 75% software and services.

Another outcome was a set of productivity measures that started improving gradually, accelerated, and became a stunning achievement. The change in business model would eventually be key to Avaya's sustainability and survival.

In the meantime, in August 2015, the market cost of high-yield debt for Avaya grew by roughly 300 basis points. This drove the company to file for Chapter 11 in January 2017 to enable a debt reorganization; this was eight years to the month after Nortel's filing, but Avaya's circumstances were quite different: Our business model was strong, and the company had been free cash flow positive in the years preceding the filing.

During the filing process, the company remained free cash flow positive and ended FY 2017 as follows:

- EBITDA as a percentage of revenue reached 26.5% for the fiscal year (another record for the business model despite being in Chapter 11).
- The mix of business for fiscal Q4 was now 82% software and service.
- Sixty-two percent of Avaya's revenue was recurring.
- Avaya's Net Promoter Score was fifty, up from forty-eight at the time of the filing and at least ten points higher than our competitors. This was odds-defying given that when companies transform, NPS usually suffers.
- The company announced that with a scheduled confirmation hearing in November 2017, we expected to emerge with half the debt and half the pension obligations, and to be on a public stock exchange by year end.

Avaya tripled its profitability over nine years, set industry-leading NPS during the transformation, and survived a $6B debt reorganization while establishing record-setting profitability, notwithstanding a level of revenue impairment during the process. In short, debt reorganization enabled by a strong business model positioned the company with a superior outcome for its capital structure. The business model was the difference maker between sustainability with a superior new capital structure and the alternate path taken by Nortel and many others.

Before we move on to the CLIMB model, it should be noted that our collective experience leading up to January 2017 felt at times like being on the end of a yo-yo string—rapid and dizzying changes, reports of progress interspersed with dire warnings of legacy obligations, and so on. Indeed, the quarter ending September 2016 was Avaya's *best quarter ever*, prior to filing Chapter 11 several months later. Understandably, the reader may experience some of that vertigo while navigating the next several chapters.

~ 5 ~

CLIMB TO THE FUTURE

When the mission to transform Avaya began in 2009, the company was in a deep hole. Whether Avaya would emerge intact and proceed to a happy ending was unpredictable, due to the variety and complexity of factors in play:

- Obligations that changed over time
  - o Pension payments
  - o Debt payments
  - o Restructuring payments
- Transformation (strategy in concert with implementation)
  - o Operational efficiencies
  - o Corporate culture
  - o Alignment of "what" with "how"
- Market dynamics
  - o Post-recession GDP trends
  - o Technology trends
  - o Competitive dynamic

In the face of such uncertainty, we implemented the CLIMB model. I had successfully used elements of this model when I was

CEO of JDS Uniphase. We transformed that company—from a -60% EBITDA/revenue to a +20% EBITDA/revenue model (2003-08), while growing the top line more than two times the size from its nadir. Although there was a clear basis on how to proceed, the model's efficacy in Avaya's unique situation was anything but certain.

To lend a bit of perspective, it is worth noting an empirical discussion by McKinsey & Co. titled "How to Beat the Transformation Odds." In 2015, McKinsey confirmed that only 26% of respondents to its Global Survey could say that their transformations had been "very or completely successful at both improving performance and equipping the organizations to sustain improvements over time." The vast majority of respondents, in other words, experienced a very different and underwhelming outcome.

A brief outline of McKinsey's model for transformation will help frame what follows. Their model features five primary stages:

a. Setting goals
b. Assessing organization capability
c. Designing transformational initiatives
d. Executing initiatives
e. Sustaining change

In addition, four practices are identified that correlate with successful transformations:

a. Communicate effectively
b. Lead actively
c. Empower employees
d. Create an environment of continuous improvement

In this regard, the CLIMB model supports the distillation of McKinsey's work. Yet the items above differ in a key aspect from the path that Avaya pursued: McKinsey's framework represents

intentions; the five stages of Avaya's CLIMB model, delineated in this chapter, are defined by **outcomes**.

At Avaya, it was essential to engage intensely, inspect regularly to ensure full accountability, and be agile enough to remediate if evidence of weekly results did not align with expectations. The aim was to create alignment among the leadership team, Board of Directors, and employees on expectations, a myriad of initiatives, and the stages of activity that would propel and sustain a journey that could take years.

The five stages of the CLIMB model are:

1. **Crisis** prompts a call to arms
2. **Leaders** are hired whose skills fit the situation
3. **Initiatives** and improvements are undertaken
4. **Metrics** define a new corporate persona and business model
5. **Benchmark** metric status is attained on multiple fronts in concert with growth.

Together, they comprise a framework for the scope of transformation, the nature of key activities and initiatives, the duration of the phases, and the anticipated outcomes from each phase. Each stage involves a teardown, then reinvention, and finally a reassembly of cross-functional processes, often requiring IT programs to implement new systems. Each phase can take a development cycle or two, which means nine to eighteen months or longer to fully implement it in a functional area.

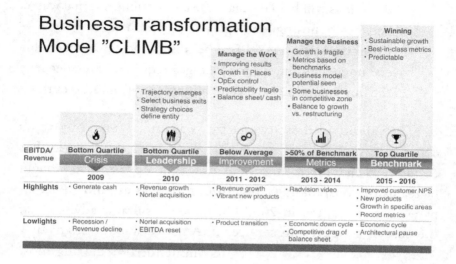

Chapter 5—Figure 1: The CLIMB Model

Let's drill down into each stage of the CLIMB model:

(1) CRISIS PROMPTS A CALL TO ARMS

Prior to my arrival, Avaya bookings had dropped precipitously, establishing the trajectory for a loss of 27% of its revenue in the first year of the Great Recession, the worst economic crisis since the 1930s. In that situation one might think it easy to galvanize the efforts of senior leaders, managers, and employees. Instead, working for their fourth CEO in three years had conditioned employees at all levels to adopt a "this too shall pass" attitude.

Reversing such long-held, self-protective attitudes demands targeted, sustained action by the leadership team. Two areas stand out in this regard:

- **Leaders must strategize and fully understand the details** of how change is going to be accomplished. Knowledge of

33

the details will help navigate the contentious internal waters between opposing ideologies or viewpoints.

- **Communication is critical** because it increases stakeholders' understanding of the changes required. This deepens the buy-in and helps ensure alignment around execution.

The validity of those two factors was underscored by Avaya's experience with initiatives *already shown to be unsuccessful*. For example, when it first went private, Avaya's new owners had brought in teams of consultants to organize initiatives around the company's cost structure. In 2007-08, these consultants advised that the cost of support and services in America was too high; they recommended offshoring most of it. When this was done, costs fell but not as much as the consultants had hoped. What *did* drop sharply was the quality of support: Customers had their calls routinely forwarded several times until they reached someone who could help. Avaya was inundated with negative feedback; customer satisfaction declined dramatically. Not surprisingly, to buy and retain the loyalty of customers in this era, front-line sales discounting moved in the wrong direction.

> *In a change environment, leaders must focus on the "how"—not just the "what."*

There were other problems, as well. The support staff in India and Argentina had attrition rates above 25%. In essence, Avaya was hiring and training people for its competitors.

Why did these things happen? Because the consultants and management team failed to focus on the "how" of making changes. Everyone learned the hard way that when you outsource complex practices, outcomes suffer. As will be discussed later, the cost structure should instead have been addressed via automation and knowledge management (i.e., systems that retrieve relevant customer history and immediately supply it to an agent or online inquiry).

Such ineffective efforts during the early privatization period understandably fomented a lack of confidence in Avaya's leadership. For the subsequent transformation, implementing CLIMB clarified the direction the company needed to head and secured the commitment of all stakeholders.

COMMUNICATION, COMMUNICATION, COMMUNICATION

As we drove change, we knew that authentic, ongoing communication was essential for making CLIMB work. The most important element in a crisis is to tell the truth so you can build trust. In both words and action, we conveyed that we were all on this journey together. We also made it clear the fix would not be quick: CLIMB's impact typically manifests in phases of twelve to eighteen months; the process does not lend itself to immediate gratification. Some changes required new IT system support, new leadership, new products to introduce change, and so on. Simply put: Achieving alignment across a variety of functions takes time.

When we started communicating, the depth of the Great Recession had not been reached. We openly stated that we did not know when the bottom would occur but that we trusted the process we were implementing—not only to ride out the storm but to thrive in spite of it.

When you are not in a position to tell people what they want to hear, frequent and transparent communication is essential. At all-hands meetings for instance, I discussed the company's current situation and took questions from the audience. I took their concerns seriously, and I gave straightforward, candid answers. This fostered transparency and trust.

More specifically, our approach to communication was rooted in advice given by the former Chairman of the Board of JDS Uniphase, Marty Kaplan: "It is impossible to overcommunicate when driving change." Marty's acronym—CUCME—became my mantra during the transformation, and is worth spelling out here:

- Communication drives understanding
- Understanding drives commitment
- Commitment drives mobilization
- Mobilization drives execution
- Execution drives success

We directed senior leaders at Avaya to conduct skip-level meetings—in which employees two or more levels removed from an executive could participate. Every employee had the opportunity to identify themselves and their role, and share observations about the company. They were invited to ask about strategy, compensation, and other issues—anything, really. These open exchanges usually went well. I took notes on how we could improve the company and communicate much better at this level of the organization. I have always believed that employees know a great deal and can, if given the right forum, provide information essential to changing the culture.

When you cannot tell people what they want to hear, frequent and transparent communication is essential.

True communication is a 360° process. Paralleling the employee meetings, I met with the Board of Directors quarterly and with executive teams on a bi-weekly and monthly basis. CLIMB fostered a communication process that reinforced what was said, what had been done, and what to expect next.

(2) LEADERS ARE HIRED TO MEET THE UNIQUE NEEDS OF THE SITUATION

As the nature of the work changed over time, stages of the CLIMB model acted as doorways for talent to enter and exit. Leaders, managers, and employees who had protected the past were replaced by new personnel who believed in and were committed to investing in the future.

We first had to hire people who could drive a path to resolution in the near-term. Hiring the *right* person for each key position proved critical to the velocity of the transformation. And since the company had to be disassembled, reinvented, and reassembled, speed mattered: Staying rooted in the past burns cash and takes focus away from the "new."

Avaya's Human Resources department worked closely with the HR experts at the private equity firms and with executive search firms to identify the most highly qualified individuals. More than once I reminded the hiring team what I'd learned from Pat Nettles, the former CEO of Ciena: "You get hired for what you know and fired for who you are." Thus, our interview process was designed to learn about the *person* we were interested in hiring, not just what he or she knew.

To guide us in this process, we analyzed the traits of leaders who were succeeding and those who were not. Certain desirable characteristics emerged to form a target lexicon, which we called the Code. It is important to add that identifying such qualities and capabilities is not a binary issue; leadership "fit" is always situational.

ELEMENTS OF THE CODE

- **Outstanding domain experience:** We looked for best-in-class executives, recognized thought leaders within certain areas of expertise, who knew what being the best would look like and were willing to help change an organization replete with employees who made excuses for not changing.

- **High Courage:** We worked hard to find leaders willing and able to take on and advance transformative goals, and systematically drive initiatives to completion.

- **Non-disruptive ego:** If a leader with an outsized ego advances an unpopular initiative that initially fails, the team may stand by and do nothing; if a leader with a non-disruptive ego advances an unpopular initiative that fails, people are more likely to help him/her forge a different path for success. The low-ego leader gets things done quietly; is not afraid to admit shortcomings or mistakes; helps others save face in difficult situations; is authentic; maximizes the contribution of all; and respects the views of others.

- **Relentless oversight:** A successful leader assigns responsibility for tasks and decisions; clearly understands and promotes objectives and measures; closely monitors process, progress, and results; weaves feedback loops into the flow; initiates daily inspections that focus on the how; and oversees the measurable status of projects.

- **Marathon-runner mindset and stamina:** Long-distance runners are comfortable when the destination is unknown. They place value in hard work and preparation; embrace challenge; are action oriented and not dissuaded by setbacks; and seize opportunities. They know how to pace themselves, sometimes falling back but maintaining a steady pace. The same applies to the best leaders in a business transformation.

- **Superior ability to hire top talent:** Successful leaders have a feel for the necessary skill sets; they are not afraid of selecting strong people; they assemble talented teams and establish a network of loyal followers. Such leaders bring in new blood that buys into the future vs. protecting the past.

- **Bias for outcomes/action:** Since new initiatives will inevitably meet resistance, strong leaders emphasize action and measurable results. They exceed goals; are consistently top performers; are aware of the bottom line; and are reliably self-motivating.
- **Teamwork and attitude:** The leaders who were succeeding at Avaya demonstrated the ability to find common ground and solve problems for the good of all with a minimum of fanfare and maximum consideration of inward and outward interests. Their ability to inspire cooperation and a team-first mentality invariably earns the trust and support of staff and peers alike.
- **Board-level mindset:** Leaders who know how to distill the complex into the simple, to maintain focus on the bottom-line, and to discern the "so what" of any situation will instill confidence and generate buy-in from the board.

When leaders failed to succeed at Avaya (before or after the transformation), the three most likely causes were outsized ego, failure to hire top talent, and not manifesting teamwork. At Avaya prior to 2009, even among the leaders who were highly intelligent and experienced, some were simply ill-equipped to contribute to cross-functional transformation—that is, to comprehend a bold new strategy and effectively bridge the "what" with the "how" of achieving new results.

(3) IMPROVEMENTS AND INITIATIVES ARE UNDERWAY

Regardless of their complexity or duration, a wide variety of improvements and initiatives were needed to transform a legacy company like Avaya. Along the way, some metrics improved while others went sideways. Teams—especially cross-functional entities—learned to adjust their execution strategy on the fly, to adapt to new metrics.

The Avaya leadership team believed that complexity was a drag on its business model, diverting focus and energy from higher priorities. So, this period required an assessment of what operations were worth improving and which should be divested to achieve simplification. One way to portray their approach to this is with two axes on a grid to show portfolio elements that can grow in revenue and EBITDA. (See Figure 2.) Note three initiatives (I_1, I_2, & I_3); the projected future state of each is indicated with an asterisk. A proper assessment might show a business's declining margins and declining revenues, with little hope of improvement, such as Initiative 2, which is a good candidate for divestiture. Over the course of nine years, Avaya divested ten businesses, simplifying the company and improving its economic model.

Improvement Prioritization Framework

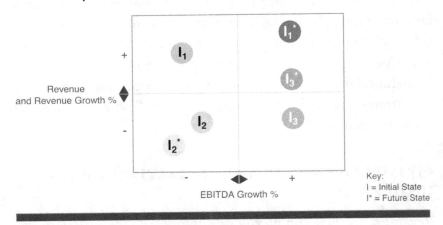

Chapter 5—Figure 2:
Improvement Prioritization Framework

The following principles defined Avaya's initial strategy for operational improvement:

1. Reduce the perimeter from negative growth and inert or materially below-target EBITDA (non-improvable) portfolio elements. Among Avaya's divestments were networking, an application server platform, test and measurement, and other services/install entities.

2. Eliminate redundancies and structural silos that cloud accountability and productivity. Organizational consolidation is key.

3. Drive key metrics of a software and services business (revenue per HC, EBITDA/HC, EBITDA%/revenue, cost per HC, fixed to variable costs shift).

4. Drive automation to reduce headcount and improve cycle time; focus on functions such as Contact Center engagement, special bids and offers, approvals, order processing, and renewals.

5. Improve quality and drive out the cost of poor quality (software, services).

6. Manage talent: Reduce cost per headcount by low-cost/high-cost management mix; shift to early experience/application focus vs. senior experience telecom focus where applicable; focus on top 30% and retention; variabilize benefits such as bonuses and even 401k matching.

7. Review core competencies and consider automating or casting off non-core, non-career aligned functions—e.g., parts of finance, parts of help desk, parts of R&D, et al.

8. Corral supplier costs: Negotiate aggressive terms and engage a minimum of two or three suppliers per strategic need.

(4) METRICS DEFINE A NEW CORPORATE PER-SONA AND BUSINESS MODEL

At this stage of the CLIMB model, generally cycle times will have improved, as will ratios normalized by headcount or revenue. Success produces metrics which, when benchmarked against industry standards, are better than the fiftieth percentile and climbing toward the top quartile.

During Stage 3 (Improvements and Innovations), Avaya focused on internal processes. Stage 4 was concentrated on growth-oriented items such as cycle time reduction and resource allocation—more specifically, systems and processes that drove superior engagement of externally focused metrics.

Furthermore, in Stage 4, new growth initiatives reveal quarter-over-quarter momentum. At Avaya, the growth of managed services, Contact Center, and application development in professional services all came into focus. Net Promoter Score also accelerated at this stage.

(5) BENCHMARK METRIC STATUS IS ATTAINED ON MULTIPLE FRONTS

As leadership progressed from managing work to managing the business, middle-managers handled the work and metrics. In this transition, talent and succession development were critical.

While outcome-oriented metrics such as customer satisfaction and NPS increasingly drove the company during this stage, in fact the company advanced in hundreds of measurements, all of which improved speed and economics.

The company achieved best-in-class in nearly all metrics. Performance was not limited to the average of top-quartile, benchmark-study achievement.

As will be seen later, Net Promoter Score (NPS) grew in importance, thanks to innovation highly prized by customers. These were largely new-revenue growth cases, and this is where our model of a software and services company was built and polished. NPS advancement and customer alignment reflected strong executive engagement on what was built, how it was delivered, and the strength of Avaya's talent to serve customers in new ways.

Financially, Avaya exited Fiscal 2016 with a record EBITDA of $940M. The total demand for products and services took an upward swing; all elements of demand for Contact Center products and services were up. EBITDA as a percentage of revenue reached a record 30% in FQ4 2016. We had released new products at a record pace, dynamic new leaders were in place, and more improvements were on the way.

~ 6 ~

VALUE CREATION COMPASS
POINTS THE WAY

With the CLIMB model in action, and a new, strong, and sustainable business model in place, we were able to guide ongoing resource allocation and investment themes by building and articulating a second model, called the Value Creation Compass (VCC). Such a model forces a leadership team to confront competitive positioning, participate in major investment themes, anticipate positioning in macro changes, and so on. It is also a useful framework for discussing divestments or a merger-and-acquisition strategy.

The VCC model is based on five thematic categories that drive value in a technology stock. (No single individual or company has authored this approach; it is but one of the numerous models devised by successful investors over time.)

VCC recognizes that any publicly traded equity or asset must intercept flows of capital investment.

Visually, the depiction of a funnel (see Fig. 1) is useful, where the circumference of the entry stretches to meet the flows of capital to the equity market and specifically to technology. The next two layers of the funnel are defined by the flows of capital to particular technology themes, followed by specific segments or categories. Finally, the size of the funnel's spout is determined by the positioning for growth of a company, followed by the quality of its financials.

The last two tiers of the model reflect largely on the intrinsic value of a company and its valuation, e.g., the long-term trading multiple based primarily on the company's financials and growth. Following is a hypothetical comparison to show the funnel's applicability.

Consider three companies that are leaders in a specific technology category. Company A is the largest of the three, is growing the fastest, and has an EBITDA/revenue of 30% with a strong balance sheet. Based on cash flows and modeling, the company may trade at a market multiple of ten times EBITDA. Company B is only 75% the size of company A, is growing a bit slower, and its business model runs at a 25% EBITDA/revenue; it trades at a valuation of eight times EBITDA. Finally, Company C is half the size of company A, has half the growth, and runs at an EBITDA/revenue of 22% with a more marginal balance sheet; Company C trades at a valuation of six times EBITDA. At some future moment, changes in the stock

> *A company that is too complex and not identified with a category or theme will likely trade at a discounted multiple.*

market occur, driving flows of dollars into the equity market, especially the technology sector. These same three companies, still running with the same financial metrics, see their stock prices move up despite no change in fundamentals. While the intrinsic values of the companies did not change (since their cash flows remain unchanged), their market valuations grew because the extrinsic value drivers picked up. Similarly, market valuations can drop in a recessionary period despite the fact that intrinsic values could stay constant.

The higher-level tier of the funnel addresses the extrinsic or vigor of the equity markets and thematic favorites. More context for each tier is provided below:

Tier 1 – Equity Market Investment Thesis: In examining the propensity of the market for investing in equities and a category of equities, are people leaving bonds and investing in technology equities? If so, a rising tide floats all boats, albeit some more than others.

Tier 2 – Market Category Investment Thesis: If the market is investing in themes or segments of technology such as telecommunication, storage, artificial intelligence, social media, et al., is there a growth theme?

Tier 3 – Company Segment Thesis: Perhaps the market is investing in a specific segment of technology—e.g., telecommunication optics vs. mobile software and services. The key here is the perception and evidence for revenue growth of companies in this segment.

Tier 4 – Company Position and Competitiveness Thesis: A key consideration is the positioning of the company: Is it the leader, a mere challenger, or one of a few companies ahead of others? The growth rate and/or nature of the top line (annuity model or one-time revenue) are critical factors.

Tier 5 – Company Financials and Operating Model: Excellent capital structure, superb business model, etc.

Categories 4 and 5 are the dominant factors that a board and a management team own and operate every day. These alone serve to differentiate a company and can increase the stock price to provide an advantage over competitors. Category 3 is vital to positioning a company strategically, such as a software and services company in a new and growing market of the future—i.e. artificial intelligence, autonomous vehicles, the Internet of Things, security, etc.

Categories 1 and 2 take prominence as investors and hedge funds move money and invest in themes. Company leadership does not control these. But when movement occurs, the stronger the positioning of categories 3, 4 and 5, the more there will be disproportionate movement in valuation and stock price. Of course, a management team does not control the stock price, but it does manage two or three of the levers of value. A leadership team needs to get these in the best possible position so that when the macro movement of investment hits their category and the equity market, the company's multiple is maximized. A company that is too complex and cannot be principally identified with a category or theme will likely trade at a discounted multiple. All the more reason to remove complexity in a company.

In short, one needs to operate for the best positioning of those levers that can be controlled and be poised to participate handsomely when the top levers find favor with investors. With that in mind, Avaya orchestrated the sale of a declining installation services business; a proprietary applications server business being run at a loss; a networking business subcritical in scale; and a test-and-measurement business that was only breaking even. Eliminating those entities reduced complexity, boosted profitability, improved the balance sheet, and positioned the company for success. Furthermore, emphasizing Avaya's investment in applications, the cloud, and managed services aligned thematically with the predominant external investment forces at the time.

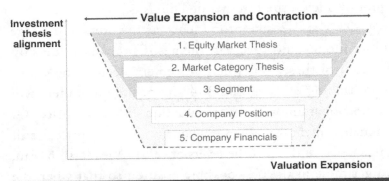

Value Creation Model

A new software and services company

Chapter 6—Figure 1: Value Creation Compass Model

With the CLIMB and the Value Creation Compass models understood, the next chapter demonstrates the transformation of Avaya from a telecom hardware company to a software and services company, by the numbers.

~ 7 ~

PEOPLE TALK, BUT NUMBERS
TELL THE TALE

Before we dive into the numbers pool, several points need to be made regarding managing expectations about the time it takes to drive change and produce true needle-moving outcomes in a larger company transformation.

First, a change in the business model will impact what customers purchase, the mix of activities, the processes and people that support those activities, and more. Frustration and resistance will increase if those involved begin the journey with unrealistic expectations about how long it may take.

In Stage 2 of the CLIMB model, new leaders are brought in who know what the change should look like. They, in turn, hire leaders to drive daily activity. At Avaya, successful change initiatives had a number of key attributes:

- There was a clear definition of current state and future state.
- Leaders of the marathon-runner style were put in place, who could absorb setbacks and remain undeterred in moving the program forward.

- The teamwork of three or more executive committee leaders drove most projects due to the need for cross-functional redefinition.

While the programs started with people-intensive activity, sustainable change occurred when new systems automated legacy work out of the company. Whereas the status quo tended to be manual, error prone, involve longer cycle times, and lack the ability to forecast, the new systems were integrative and capable of forecasting and scaling naturally with changes in demand.

Automation took time to define, execute, and transition, but once accomplished, the new business was healthier, more fun for the employees, and produced better service for customers.

A pivotal decision for the success of long-term transformation was the establishment of the Chief Restructuring Officer role (as noted in Chapter 2). CRO Jim Chirico and his team infused a constant prioritization and focus upon systems and process change to drive automation, cycle time, et al. Measurements, inspection, and analytics kept the categories of initiatives and the overall amalgam on track. When obstacles were confronted, the know-how from other "how to" discoveries was shared with teams attempting change for the first time.

The change process involved hundreds of detailed processes, activities, and metrics. Avaya challenged itself to improve year-over-year by attaining and surpassing best-in-class performance levels. For example, under inventory management, the evolution was from less than five to ten or more turns. Inventory turns is the ratio of how many times a company's inventory is sold and replaced within a specified period. The higher the ratio, the lower the risk and the better the business model.

The devil's in the details.

The accomplishment numerically eclipsed a 100% improvement in the metric.

The work across many hundreds of metrics drove change that improved the use of cash, lowered operational risk, and generally improved service to customers. Over time, the evolution of those myriad items began to move the major metrics such as productivity, EBITDA/revenue, gross margins, et al., eventually achieving the critical mass needed for transformation.

As noted earlier, the recession of 2008-09 was a severe assault on the company's business plan. The single largest revenue stream, Unified Communications, is the type of business that grows when Gross Domestic Product (GDP) is above 2.5% and contracts when GDP falls below the same threshold. In fact, in 2009 roughly 60% of the company's profits were concentrated in several hundred enterprise customer accounts. Many of these accounts were hit hard by the Great Recession or by decisions to consolidate with their rivals, shrinking the market. In Avaya's book of business, banks, pharmaceutical companies, and the federal government all reduced spending at that time.

Figure 1 shows the correlation of the company's revenue trending with GDP movement, and specifically the absence of growth when GDP trends below 2.5%. However, not shown here is the fact that in the sixteen years prior to 2007, there were nine years where annual GDP growth eclipsed 2.5%, half of those years being close to 4%. So, the era of 2008-16 was significantly muted in terms of GDP and the opportunity associated with it.

In short, relative to the initial Avaya business plan, there were several major assumptions that had not been foreseen:

- A recession.
- A recession that drove GDP in 2009 to -2.8%.
- A GDP environment that was substantially muted for roughly a decade from 2008 to 2018 versus the sixteen years prior.

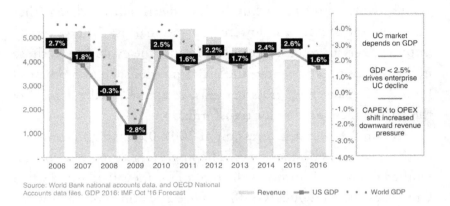

Avaya Total Revenue & GDP Trend

Source: World Bank national accounts data, and OECD National Accounts data files. GDP 2016: IMF Oct '16 Forecast

Revenue ■ US GDP • • • World GDP

Chapter 7—Figure 1: Avaya Total Revenue and GDP Trend

Fearing that GDP growth post-2009 might not reach the levels of, say, 2005 and 2006, we firmly believed that operational transformation would be the cornerstone to survival. In other words: Failure to push productivity while revenues were falling would result in debt service and other obligations eventually swallowing the company.

Figure 2 shows numerically the yield of the transformation work. While the GDP trending worked against top line advancement, adjusted EBITDA grew from $753M in F2009 to $940M in F2016. Operating income grew year-over-year from roughly $500M in F2007 to $756M in F2016—a 50% improvement in absolute terms and a doubling as percent of revenue.

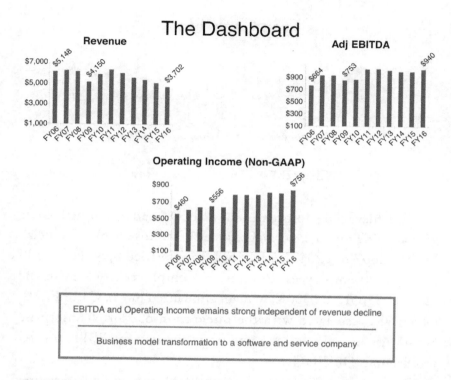

Chapter 7—Figure 2: Revenue, EBITDA, Operating Income

GAAP free cash flow was pressured by debt service, pension service, and restructuring service increases. All three were costlier than the original take-private business plan assumed, due to the depth of the recession (volume of subsequent restructuring), debt service (due to ongoing amend and extend cycles and debt costing incrementally more each time it was renewed), and pension costs (which grew since the interest rate was low and pension funding increases when interest rate yields are lower). Nevertheless, Avaya was free cash flow positive for three of the four years leading up to F2016. See Figure 3.

Free Cash Flow

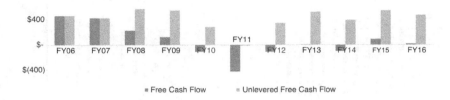

Chapter 7—Figure 3: Cash Flow

To achieve the improvement of EBITDA and operating income with a falling top line, normalized metric improvement was crucial. In the F2007 to F2011 period, headcount varied between 15,500 and 18,700 employees. Revenue per employee hovered in the range of $265K to $300K, with an annualized low in Q1 of F2010 of $209K, associated with the integration of Nortel Enterprise Solutions. At roughly the same time, the low for EBITDA/HC was around $38K/HC.

By the end of F2016 (September 2016), the annualized figures of merit were roughly $100K/HC for EBITDA attainment and $370K/HC for revenue attainment. By that time, Avaya's headcount was around 10,000 with a dramatically different mix of business as a new software and services company. Automation, outsourcing, and asset divestiture were important enablers in improving productivity.

CAPITAL STRUCTURE IN PERSPECTIVE

The debt structure of a take-private company is typically reviewed relative to its current and projected cash flows. However, it is typical for the ratio identified as the net debt/EBITDA to fall in a range from 5 to 7. When Avaya was taken private, this ratio in F2008 was 5.6. With the revenue declines of the recession and the purchase of Nortel Enterprise Solutions, the ratio increased to 7.0. In the years following, the ratio improved to 6.0 in F2016. While this ratio marked the midpoint of a range typical at the outset of a go-private transaction, it also represented a lack of delevering versus what had been anticipated at the beginning of the go-private capital structure.

Unfortunately, the need to restructure more, pay more pension service, and pay more debt service over the course of a decade prevented the company from aggressively delevering its balance sheet (notwithstanding the decline of revenue, which did not help). Said another way, the increased costs of pension obligations, restructuring in the wake of the recession, and debt service cost increases conflated to consume capital that would otherwise have been deployed to delever further.

To place these forces in perspective, legacy obligations consumed more than $6.7B in the years from F2008 to F2016. The cumulative pension service paid was roughly $1.42B. The cumulative debt service paid eclipsed $3.9B. Given the required scope of transformation in the wake of a deep recession, the cumulative restructuring expenses in this same period totaled more than $1.32B. This $6.7B legacy obligation represented $2.7B more than what was comprehended at the outset of the go-private transition. In other words, the advent and wake of the recession deprived the capital structure of roughly $2.5B of delevering or the achievement of net debt/EBITDA below 4.0 by the end of F2016.

THE BUSINESS MODEL

To bring the transformation into greater clarity, Figure 4 provides a summary of the business in FQ4 2016 and for F2016. By the end of FQ4 2016, with its business converted to a software and services company, Avaya achieved record metrics. The continued drive for productivity—through automation, new product innovation, and the advancement of an improved mix of business toward value-based software and services—enabled an ongoing ascent of EBITDA, operating income, and the overall business model.

The Business (FQ4'16, FY16)

Performance Metrics	Q4 Fy15	Q4 FY16	FY15	FY16
Period Revenue	$1,008M	$958M	$4,081M	$3,702M
Annualized Revenue Run Rate	$4.0B	$3.8B	$4.1B	$3.7B
Annualized Revenue per Employee	$347K	$380K	$347K	$356K
Product Gross Margin (%)	65%	64%	63%	64%
Services Gross Margin (%)	59%	60%	58%	59%
Total Gross Margin (%)	62%	62%	61%	62%
EBITDA (%)	24%	30%	22%	25%
EBITDA	$246M	$284M	$900M	$940M
Software & Services % of Revenue	72%	74%	71%	75%
Net Promoter Score*	54	58	56	58

Record Metrics

Note: All amounts as reported
* Four quarter rolling average

Chapter 7—Figure 4: The Business (Q4 FY2015, FY2016)

The darkened matrix elements highlight the records set by Avaya: Revenues per employee of $380K, EBITDA margins of 30%, a software and services mix of 74%-75%, and an NPS of 58 all demonstrate a highly productive company. Of course, some areas still required remediation, mostly on the go-to-market side.

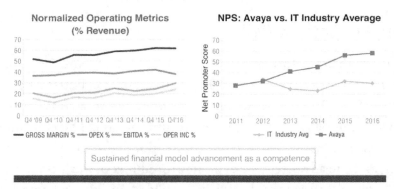

The Outcomes
Historical Non - GAAP Trends

Sustained financial model advancement as a competence

Chapter 7—Figure 5: Historical Non-GAAP Trends

With these trends now placed on a single chart (Figure 5), Avaya's needle-moving numerical journey is displayed. As revenues dropped, the adjusted EBITDA percent expanded, enabling ongoing profit to pay for the increased cost of legacy obligations. Normalized operating metrics hit benchmark levels, most notably EBITDA/revenue of 30% and operating income of 24%. As revenue dropped, so did headcount, at a rate constrained by the automation speed of outsourcing of non-core activity; by the divestiture of underperforming assets; and by the deployment of dollars for restructuring.

Perhaps most noteworthy, Avaya's Net Promoter Score continued to climb as the company transformed and its technology changed. NPS measures loyalty and responds to innovation, so even in an industry that was rapidly moving to recurring revenue models, Avaya's score of 58 was 20 points or more above its nearest competitor and 30 points higher than the average of the IT industry. Later we will discuss several learnings based on this transformation.

Many companies in the software and services world were struggling with their top-line demand because consumption models were switching from one-time models to OPEX (operating expense) or subscription models paid over time. In Avaya's case, total demand stayed roughly flat when measured by the sum of one-time revenue and distributed over time as committed revenue. However, the quarterly reported revenue dropped for some time.

On the other hand, Avaya's Contact Center business evidenced growing demand over time, demonstrating healthy growth and an even stronger business model than the company as a whole.

In summary, what the numbers convincingly portray is a legacy firm that changed its underlying business model in dramatic fashion by disassembling the past and reinventing both the product portfolio and its operations. *How* Avaya did this is detailed in the following chapters, beginning with the transformation of its culture.

~ 8 ~

TRANSFORMING THE CULTURE

Initially, at the beginning of 2009, the mission to drive the company to far greater levels of productivity was not received as a clarion call by most employees. The fact that I was their fourth CEO in three years did not help.

Culture can be a dramatic inhibitor to change. After years of working in a legacy culture, many employees at Avaya had been unwittingly conditioned in one of two ways: Some viewed themselves as survivors waiting to see what would happen and how it might affect their jobs. Others bet that the new guy in charge, like previous CEOs, could not create sustained change; some even actively subverted the agenda for change.

The mission to drive far greater levels of productivity was not received as a clarion call by most employees.

Nonetheless, Avaya leadership believed and began to communicate that crisis equals opportunity. The CLIMB model and other initiatives allowed the executive team to set expectations and to describe, function by function, how to create results that would "move the needle." The CLIMB model sent the message that the executive team had done this work successfully before; they anticipated the challenges and were prepared for the long haul. Supported by metrics at each stage of the transformation and with progress reports communicated regularly, the numbers emboldened supporters and skeptics alike and began to transform the culture.

A few anecdotes will illustrate the point:

"PROBLEMATIC EXECUTIVES"

During my first week at Avaya, I went to the Customer Briefing Center. I requested the briefing given to the most recent customer. I found it to be lacking in customer-use case knowledge, technical proficiency and significance. The presentation was given by a professional briefer rather than someone responsible for the products and solutions being sold. I asked how many customers received such briefings and was told thousands per year. Then I inquired how many of my direct reports gave presentations to customers. The answer was "very few," because the Briefing Center wanted to *protect the customers from the executive team.* I was stunned by this. The explanation? Executives caused problems—including leaving in the middle of briefings, overcommitting on projects, and getting customers excited about new products. In short, there was an attitude of protecting customers from unfulfilled expectations.

"FEAR AND INERTIA"

After peeling back the onion of Avaya operations, it became apparent that our Contact Center had roughly 40% of our employee base as agents, at 200 sites around the world. This represented an enormous cost, and with only 4% of support calls being handled by online access, the model was out of step with our competitors. Moreover, customer satisfaction was moving in the wrong direction, especially during the period when jobs were offshored. Among the top complaints from customers were: It took too long to reach a knowledgeable person; often the agents did not know the products; and, after waiting up to an hour on hold, customers were told that the company had been aware of the problem for months!

In response, we developed a plan to segment the customer inbound calls and provide self-service to those who could most quickly get answers online.

As we began this process, numerous groups within the company openly disdained the effort to provide more self-service.

To illustrate how devious the opposition could be, one day I received letters from four clergymen (each from a different religious affiliation) in the Denver area, where there was a concentration of agents. Each letter had the same message: Avaya must not modernize the Contact Center because jobs might be lost. When I examined the envelopes, all four had the same return address—a union assembly hall outside of Denver.

The next week I visited the executive vice president of sales of one of our large channel partners. During a review of our relationship with them, he told me that while Avaya's products worked well, our customer support was poor. He said that his direct reports had reached out to the Contact Center for help and were told on numerous occasions that agents wouldn't assist them because they feared losing their jobs.

After waiting up to an hour on hold, customers were being told that the company had been aware of the problem for months.

When I returned to Avaya headquarters, I requested that our leadership team follow up to confirm whether what I'd heard was true. The first response they received from agents was that it never happened. I told the team that customers provide feedback to make us better and we should double-check the data. We then placed voice recording on agent calls and learned that indeed this kind of response occurred 7.5% of the time. Appropriate individuals were given disciplinary action. It stopped quickly.

Both the clergy letters and the poor response to customer concerns demonstrated the sophistication of effort to protect jobs and preserve the past. Some readers might recall the Luddites, a group of English textile workers and weavers in the early nineteenth century who destroyed weaving machinery, fearing that the machines would replace them and their skills. It's human nature. This tension between human capital in the future of work and the advancement of productivity with artificial intelligence will continue and increase in import as companies digitally transform.

"DISINCENTIVES"

At one time, on a relatively old Avaya product, the cost of engineering was high and the quality of the code was quite poor. Defects were higher with this product than almost any other in our portfolio. Upon examination, our head of Research & Development found that the development team had outsourced current engineering and paid that firm per "bug" or "defect" fixed. As one might surmise, the unwitting outcome here is that the more defects the firm created, the more money they got and the more people they could employ. Amazingly, Avaya's legacy culture had created a contract that encouraged non-value-added work.

Unfortunately, there were many stories like these. They are often counterintuitive if you think about how things *should* work. The lesson here is that automating and transforming a company threatens those who are resistant to change, but it is necessary to mechanize out poor customer experiences.

In a change environment, a leadership team must focus on the "how," not just the "what." Focusing on the "how" makes visible the difference between wrong and right behaviors, as with a minority of the Contact Center agents. Once the outcome was measured per call and the evidence of the wrongdoing was available daily, those employees not doing it correctly were persuaded to change.

This was also true when trying to drive software quality to levels that were superior to our competitors. Measurement, prediction, and true performance were made public and employees responded. Only personal risk and personal and team rewards overcame the culture of adverse choices. Successful transformation requires directly accountable individuals, enabled by measurement and metrics.

In a growth company, a culture that values participation encourages alignment of team members naturally. They more willingly accept what is asked of them and figure out how to do something better, and faster.

In the resistant culture that existed at Avaya before 2009, unrealized execution consumed strategy or the "what" every day. I felt it would be wise to spend more time with people who are not entitled. Ensuring the appropriate "how" was essential. Incubating growth separate from restructuring is a crucial organizational approach.

Vital to all of this is the leadership. The intent of the next chapter is to frame the imperative for hiring the most compelling and gifted situational leaders, i.e., those who possess the most suitable set of talents for the dismantling of the past and reinvention of the future.

~ 9 ~

THE RIGHT LEADERSHIP

In the transformation of a company that has elements of entitlement in its culture, hiring the right leadership is vital. Bringing in a "star" executive from a growth company who believes he/she can give orders that will be executed flawlessly, will inevitably fail and thus fuel the regeneration of entitlement.

Indeed, the most effective leaders in any situation should *expect* to fail, at times: "No pain, no gain," as the saying goes. The difference is what they do when setbacks occur. I recall a family vacation when our kids were much younger, in which I found myself about to launch from the precipice of a sand dune near Kitty Hawk, North Carolina, strapped into a hang glider. The young instructor's simple directions echoed in my ear: "Stand up, start running, and leap!" Within milliseconds, I face-planted into the slope of the dune. Moments later, the instructor offered this clarification: "Hey, pops—this ain't lawn darts!" My pride was the only thing injured; I knew I'd be hearing this

> *Organizational transformation will test an executive's ability like no other opportunity.*

story re-told by my wife and kids for years. But I climbed back up that dune, to try again.

As you might expect, during the uncertainty and non-commonplace activities of Avaya's transformation, we needed "low ego, high courage" leaders who had demonstrated the ability to put their pride aside long enough to learn from failure or adversity, get up, and keep going.

It will be helpful to look at what leaders in a transformation are required to do. First, they must conceive and build a path to the future while weaning the status quo. To assess a leader's impact on individual employees, consider the spectrum of individuals on two axes, as in Figure 1, below.

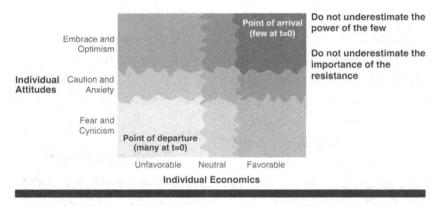

Chapter 9—Figure 1: The Transformation Culture Shift: Leadership Challenge

The first axis (vertical) considers an individual's attitude about change, which can be seen in variations of fear and cynicism, cautious anxiety, and optimistic embrace, recognizing that the fear and cynicism brings strong resistance. The second axis (horizontal) is an individual's perception of the personal economic benefit of change and transformation, ranging (left to right) from degrees of unfavorable, to neutral, to degrees of favorable.

At the point of departure for a new transformation, there exists a majority of employees in the lower left quadrant—that is, individuals who generally fear change as well as the potential personal impact of change. In the upper right quadrant, with a view of what their future and thus the point of arrival might look like, is a small number of leaders (perhaps reinforced by consultants who assist in priming the pump of change). At the outset, new leaders face the challenge of driving new outcomes despite being significantly outnumbered, sometimes by as much as 1,000 to 1.

For this reason, systems that help break down the work and drive force-multipliers or leverage in accelerating change are crucial. Some of these elements of leverage might include:

- Divesting complexity so more focus can be applied to the core business.
- Outsourcing non-core business to organizations and engaging external partners in driving required model change.
- IT systems that drive new and simplified automated processes.
- New measurement systems and metrics that bring accountability to individuals and teams on a daily basis.
- Use of a few highly potent consultants who provide the tooling for decision support and incubation of success pilots to prove transformation will work.

In short, leadership in a company undergoing transformation has the obligation to comprehend that at the outset (t=0), they begin their mission with a strategy and a set of initiatives but must pull individuals and the culture along to support the future state. To do this when the legacy greatly outnumbers the new, requires systems and leverage. What we observed is reflected above in Figure 1:

Some bright, capable leaders did not have what it took to succeed at Avaya. Those lost opportunities drove us to look carefully at the traits associated with leaders who achieved "move the needle" outcomes. We assembled nine traits and used them to guide the hiring of new executives. While not applicable to all leaders of all businesses in all situations, these qualities proved essential to driving the numbers discussed earlier. The traits have been discussed in an earlier chapter, but are enumerated here as reference:

1. Outstanding domain expertise
2. High courage
3. Non-disruptive ego
4. Relentless inspection
5. A metaphorical marathon runner
6. Superior ability to hire top talent
7. A bias for outcomes and action
8. Teamwork and attitude
9. Board-level mindset

None of these traits will surprise experienced business people. What is unique is the heavy emphasis we placed on them and our determination that other characteristics are less important to long-term transformation. They provide a guide to hiring executives who can succeed in a complex environment in which executing a plan to disassemble the past and innovate for the future requires ambidextrous capabilities. They also help reveal when a leader is not performing well during a transformation effort, and why he or she might need to transition from the company.

ACCOUNTABILITY AND EXCELLENCE

As part of our strategy to infuse hiring with maximum effect and efficiency, we hired an executive coach, Tom Steitz, the former US ski team coach of a gold-medal winning program and team, to drive the individual and collective success of the executive team.

As part of his process, Tom employed a twice-annual climate survey to gauge whether executives were aligning with increasing cohesiveness or if the team or individuals were splintering in some way. When splintering became evident, there would be a period to support an executive, but if the assistance was rejected and the executive was unable to change course, then he or she was separated from the business. Interestingly, over almost nine years, numerous executives transitioned out who resisted, or who mistakenly felt they were doing well and had the executive team 100% behind them, or who felt that the splintering should not matter. The lesson here: When outsized ego takes center stage, it's often a sign that self-awareness is low and needs to be addressed.

Beyond that, the most frequent causes of a leader not being a good "fit" to execute the transition were: (1) lack of ability to either hire an effective team or make his or her team productive and creative; (2) lack of commitment to teamwork; or (3) lack of self-awareness, and ego issues. Ultimately, the speed of transformation depends on getting the right leadership in place who can both define the "how to" of change and put in place people who can help ensure the future of the company.

CHANGE AGENTS

Finding and hiring outstanding executives is one thing. Coming on board during an organizational transformation will test any executive's ability to *lead a team in effecting change* in an extreme circumstance.

Employees have any number of perceptions and motivations about the work they do; many identify closely with their jobs; most are highly dependent on the income they earn; some are attached to the space they occupy and the people they associate with every day. The prospect of change is unsettling; the reality of change often contributes to a fear of being devalued.

> *The most effective leaders should expect to fail, at times.*

We observed that successful leaders recognize and deal with such feelings proactively. The ability to listen, be authentic, communicate clearly, and provide positive, constructive feedback, are all signs of a successful *change agent*. Such individuals are in the minority, unfortunately, and it was the Avaya leadership team's responsibility to find leaders with those capabilities, develop them, and ensure they had the support to succeed.

LEADERS AND SYSTEMS

Along the way, we discovered one other vital trait for successful transformational leadership: the ability to create change by establishing new systems that reinforced the metrics, execution, and predictability of future outcomes. Leaders who limited their efforts to simply defining the "what" and hiring a few new managers, rarely reached best-in-class. Those who built new systems and changed how Avaya operated cross-functionally, typically achieved maximum speed and impact. We saw this in customer service, in cost of quality improvement, and finally, in the success of changing inventory management turns and supply chain management.

Systems matter for sustainable performance. This becomes more evident through one of the most counterintuitive companion accomplishments in the transformation of Avaya—the dramatic ascent of the company's Net Promoter Score.

~ 10 ~

INNOVATION AND NET PROMOTER SCORE

From the beginning of the transformation work, Avaya's leadership team committed to becoming a recognized innovator in the solutions it sold—i.e., investing in innovation and operational remediation that was meaningful to customers and partners. I used to tell my team that if we weren't innovating—if we couldn't give customers something they could get *only* from Avaya—we weren't doing our job and we didn't deserve their business. In other words, companies are best served by cultivating a customer-pull environment. This is especially true when a company is restructuring itself, because internal dynamics tend to take on a life of their own.

Two examples of such dynamics are: (a) In 2010-11, our customers began to ask for a service that proactively managed day-to-day outcomes provided by Avaya Technology. Internal resistance at Avaya cropped up immediately. Nonetheless, the leadership team persisted in directing changes to meet those customers' demands (and, in the process, generated a new revenue stream); initial success in this effort soon overcame the resistance. (b) Around the same time, we created a work flow automation engine for the Unified

Communications portfolio. Again, initially there was push-back inside, but the customers adopted the technology and responded with loyalty. Both of those delivered Net Promoter Scores in excess of 60.

What was not fully understood at the outset was (1) the interaction between innovation and Net Promoter Score (NPS); (2) the magnitude of change that was possible; and (3) which decisions would enable the greatest advancement.

By way of a reminder, NPS is a specific form of tool that enables a company to gauge the satisfaction of customers, or more specifically, their loyalty. Typically (and this was true in Avaya's case), a third party asks questions of customers and partners. Responses can be given from zero to ten and the Net Promoter Score is provided in a range from -100 to 100. In the technology sector, as will be shown later, an average score would be in the 20s while typically the best of the best consumer companies are in the top 1% with scores above 70.

After the acquisition of Nortel Enterprise Solutions in 2010, external discontent was widespread. Concerns over which products would continue going forward, operational integration issues, software quality issues, et al. provided Avaya with a clear mandate to focus on the customer. The combined businesses also revealed warring internal factions, each seeking survival. Customers saw this shadow cast over the company, and rightfully felt that they deserved better. To address that critical issue, the company had undertaken the measurement of NPS; in one specific quarter the index was at 14.

To the executive team, an NPS of 14 was both undesirable and unsustainable. In much the same way that the company had employed the CLIMB model to manage expectations around the journey of transformation, the leadership team implemented the same five-phase plan or lexicon to drive a significant and sustainable uplift in NPS. Recognition that the status quo was unacceptable came to define and propel an internal sense of crisis, which drove a consensus that the culture of the company had to focus on being pulled by customers and partners (the first step of the CLIMB model).

The next step was to ensure we had a leader and a structure for prioritizing and launching initiatives that would improve alignment with customers; enable identification and measurement of the improvement initiatives; ensure that measurement drove accountability to individual teams; and ultimately to significantly alter execution. At this point we asked a highly capable individual, Jerry Glembocki, to drive process improvement since he and his team had already achieved success in driving cross-functional support for episodic customer issues. Jerry assembled a team of specialists with domain knowledge and Lean quality training, who succeeded in resolving problems for dozens of critical accounts. Major attention was also given to software quality improvements; the cost of quality dropped from around $800M in 2010-11 to less than $180M in 2016.

Next came the identification and operationalization of initiatives. Given the scoring mentioned above, there existed a target rich environment. To add context for the reader, here is a brief list of the nature of the issues:

- concerns over product roadmap communication and clarity;
- concerns over product development dates sliding;
- first releases of software had too many reported troubles; and
- slow support response (taking too long to be handed off to the right expert).

As might be expected, some issues were clear process issues (upfront specification and documentation of a solution or managed service). Some involved the quality of actual work (e.g., bugs in the software) and their inherent disciplines. On the positive side, using customer input and measurement, Jerry and the team guided the company in addressing the issues that meant the most to customers—well over a hundred initiatives. Both remediation and innovation emerged as team members and line management increasingly made progress that drove the metrics in their areas of accountability. The result was a dramatic improvement in the Net Promoter Score. These initiatives created an impetus for ongoing improvement.

Several important examples are worth noting:

1. Innovation: Avaya's rich history of innovation had become somewhat threadbare in the tech world approaching 2010. Fresh competition from Cisco, Microsoft, and low-end cloud players was having a disruptive effect. This reality stood in stark contrast to the dynamic that had existed in the traditional business telecom space, in which a growing enterprise would expand and upgrade their software with a predictable set of metrics. Prior to the 2008 recession, that predictable pattern of churn for the aggregate of business customers might have been 8% to 14% per year. Once the recession arrived, the pattern was broken.

When it became clear that the pattern could not continue, our response was to personally visit with business leaders of our customers and ask them what we could expect going forward. In my first of forty interviews, I asked Wendell Weeks, CEO of Corning, when he planned to upgrade the technology of his PBX software and phone system. His answer was unequivocal: "Never." They had *no plan to upgrade the past.* I then asked what he *did* plan to spend money on; his response included: mobile, video, networking, security, bring-your-own device, et al.

Change or die.

This conversation virtually repeated itself more than thirty times. The lesson was unmistakable: With missionary zeal, Avaya needed to drive innovation and differentiation from the top down, while also allowing the customer inbound to pull Avaya. Product innovation needed to *intercept* new categories of spend. As Alexander Graham Bell said: "When one door closes, another opens. But we often look so long and so regretfully upon the closed door that we do not see the one which has opened for us."

Over the next five years, the company invested heavily in R&D in addition to executing three or four modest acquisitions per year. To become the recognized specialist in communications—i.e., Bell's "open door"—Avaya emphasized developments that were focused on:

- software innovation and virtualization;
- all channels of communication (voice, video, and data);
- simplicity that reduced the burdens of install and support versus competitors;
- emphasis on applications and services over infrastructure; and
- managed services, subscription procured services, and cloud deployment models.

In essence, the company developed an application-centered infrastructure. In this infrastructure, application programming interfaces enabled events to trigger and dynamically initiate communication streams, subject to customer policies.

Some examples will help clarify this:

1. A customer has a security surveillance vendor that senses a breach. The security appliance sends a message to the communications server to dynamically isolate the network address where the breach occurred by communicating with the SDN routing appliance. At the same time, Unified Communications notifies seven accountable company leaders that they're required to join a video call that has been scheduled for a discussion of the breach. Thus,

automation across heretofore isolated technology solutions enabled immediate response and escalation without human intervention.

2. A new generation of vehicle offers unique user experiences. The support team asks for an application that will accept input from their surveillance of a deployed vehicle whose tire is losing air. They need an application that can take the input, send a text message or place a call to alert the driver, provide information on the closest location for assistance, and possibly stay on the line until the problem is resolved. In less than an hour the application flow was developed, and it was deployed in less than three days.

In both examples, the innovation was unique and the ability to serve a customer's business needs for their own differentiation was clear.

2. Quality: The Avaya research team used an array of software best practices and methodology to create a model. They found that over a long period of time, more than 90% of the problems typically resided in a very few modules of code. The weak links drove the majority of the customer-observed problems.

Next, after empirically modeling the performance of teams and their compliance with best practices and the numerical indications of pre-released testing, such as unit testing, integration testing, and system testing, they were able to predict the likelihood that software would be superior in quality, average, or below target. In short, a tool was invented to predict the customer experience and therefore guard against both episodic surprises and a poorly trending organization. Bottom line: Software quality improved dramatically over the next five years.

The impact of this work improved on-time delivery of software products, higher customer satisfaction because intrinsic quality was better, and fewer resources spent fixing problems. During a focus on improving cost of quality, this do-it-right-the-first-time innovation eliminated tens of millions of dollars per year of rework.

3. Support: Although this subject will be discussed in more detail later, its relevance to a key important customer complaint makes it worth mentioning here. During the first two years of customer visits it was common to hear that Avaya had superb talent, but when a customer called for help, they were often routed to between four and eight people who each seemed to know very little. Even more frustrating, the last person reached would tell the customer that the problem had been known for six months and documented someplace that very few people knew about. This customer service merry-go-round was completely unacceptable.

Under the leadership of Mike Runda, the company took a number of innovative steps. First, it began the move to web enablement for support—i.e., customer self-service. Second, when a customer service agent resolved an issue, it was newly required to be published within thirty minutes for all to see. Individual agents loved this because they no longer needed to search for a solution that had already been found. Support engineers were working on new issues more frequently. For customers, they could find what was already known immediately and then be routed to a real subject matter expert more quickly. The speed and cost of service was improved for both the customer and Avaya.

The company also segmented the customer base with processes tailored for the very largest customers, highly sensitive customers, the mid-market, and so forth.

In the next chapter, we will see that the move to self-service improved the company's cost structure materially. Just as important, more engaged support personnel delivering answers more quickly benefited customers, and as a result our NPS jumped as much as ten points just from those efforts.

What was most important through all that was the learning and the numbers. The impact of Avaya's investment in new innovation and an emphasis on delighting customers can be seen in Figure 1: The Net Promoter Score journey.

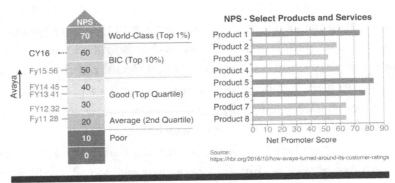

The Outcomes
NPS Journey

Chapter 10—Figure 1: Net Promoter Score Journey

First, by the end of September 2016, the company had reached an NPS of 58, an impressive 28 points above the aggregate industry average. It was clear to Avaya team members and customers that the company had learned to listen to customers and had an organizational capability to sustainably improve its alignment across many fronts. The company had achieved differentiation from its competitors.

Second, the initial work on remediation had moved our NPS into the high 20s or low 30s. This work made the company more efficient and also saved money. It was a win for customers and for the company on many fronts.

Third, as new product innovation was brought to market that had been aligned with customers from the get-go, these products and services were often achieving NPS from the high 50s to mid-70s, a zone of excellence that had the added benefit of significantly moving the corporate averages up to the high 50s.

Fourth, it was clear that having customers pull the company brought recognition from other customers as well as from industry-award bodies. Simply remediating things will move the NPS only so far. Bringing innovation to the market to solve urgent problems for customers generates even stronger NPS movement, as customers are more likely to recommend the firm's products and services.

Avaya's Net Promoter Score continued to climb as the company transformed and its technology changed.

That point has been affirmed in a McKinsey study where the new digital interfaces of applications of new economy banking (e.g., employing mobile channels) brings much greater NPS than legacy banking experiences.

During the entire focus on NPS ascent, the status was monitored by a third party and reviewed monthly by the Avaya leadership team. Fairly granular data existed per sales region, product, or service category, etc. Over time, an increasing percentage of issues was based in process management and speed of response in specific regions.

All of the above activities conspired to improve the experience of speed as well as to place pressure on Avaya to automate, and to improve processes and systems.

Looking back, the NPS mission accomplished five things:

- improved culture and moved the focus to the outside looking in;
- forced a focus on systems that in turn increased the speed of execution of overall transformation;

- increased the focus on innovation and a higher level of customer relevance;
- improved new customer wins and increased retention; and
- favorably assisted financial productivity metrics.

The investment in innovation was essential to finding growth in transitioning markets. During the period through 2016, the following elements of growth had been nurtured.

- The Unified Communications and Contact Center's infrastructure became software-based and programmable, redefining work flows for customers. The Contact Center's business had grown to be in excess of $1B with best-in-class operating margins. This business was growing at a yearly pace of high single-digit percent.
- New businesses, such as session border controllers, custom application to support programmable work flows, and new software assurance models, each contributed from $50M/year to more than $150M/year.
- The organically developed managed-services business had grown to contribute more than $300M/year of top-line relevance.
- The secure software-defined networking product suite had been selected by more than 1,000 enterprise customers with revenue contribution exceeding $150M/year.
- Initially, cloud and subscription models and revenue were introduced for adoption.

These threads of growth were clear and were pulling the company. The power of innovation, quality, and support to drive improvement in the Net Promoter Score was entirely dependent on the systems thinking and measurement tools that are the subject of the next chapter.

~ 11 ~

SYSTEMS THINKING AND DIGITAL TRANSFORMATION

One aspect of the transformation of a telecom hardware company to a software and services company was that the speed of action had to move much more quickly and in alignment with people and events both inside and outside of Avaya. Many aspects of waste and a lack of predictability had to be addressed.

To take just one example, in the years 2009 and 2010 the probability that an ordered product would arrive on schedule was approximately 55% of the time. If an order required four items to be delivered on time for a solution to be deployed, this simultaneous event would occur on time 55% to the fourth power or roughly 9% of the time. Because of such poor execution, customer satisfaction was low. As mentioned before, our NPS circa 2010 was at its lowest level—around 14.

After the 2010 era, new leadership began to organize the supply chain and to add predictive software, specifically a software tool called Kinaxis. By the end of 2016, on-time shipments occurred roughly 98% of the time or better.

OPERATIONAL CUL-DE-SACS

People like to live in neighborhood cul-de-sacs: They are generally quiet, due to the lack of through traffic, and they engender a sense of belonging and safety among those who live there. But in the world of business, an operational cul-de-sac is usually detrimental, and can be deadly: They are by definition comfortable and familiar, limiting one's view to what's worked in the past, no matter how anachronistic or self-defeating. During the Avaya transformation this involved people and manual processes. Two examples:

- leaders who resisted the movement to customer self-service despite the reality that customers could obtain self-service with Avaya's competitors; and
- leaders who chose to ignore unacceptable service intervals for a few customers if the aggregate statistics looked OK—i.e., the pain of individual customers would be rationalized away by the averages.

Many believed that the rhythm of the business prior to the recession was going to return post-recession. All that was required was to wait. This was the deception of the "churn" rate history that was discovered, through customer interviews, to be irrelevant. The reality is that in the wake of a recession or major bubble-cycle bursting, what customers bought before the episode will nearly always be replaced by new preferences and economics due to innovation. Assuming that the past will recover is perilous.

> *Cul-de-sacs limit one's view to what has worked in the past, no matter how anachronistic or self-defeating.*

Operational excellence became a critical goal during the transformation. Given the numerical factors that framed the company in the wake of the Great Recession, operational excellence was not merely a choice—it was the only path to survival. It was essential to pay the bills or the company's runway would have been foreshortened, perhaps fatally. However, since a claim to operational excellence can sound like a cliché, it may help to mention the factors that made Avaya's pursuit of it unique:

- Scale: It was a large, $4B+ revenue company with extraordinarily deep legacy roots.
- With the invention of new models and processes, the scale of new measurements to be embraced, implemented, and optimized was enormous. The gravitational pull to continue using measurements of the past was very strong. How you measure, how you structure organizations to disassemble the past and reinvent a future, and how you structure initiatives that take you to a future, step by step, require uncommon skills. Leaders satisfied with "just run the business" or a one-dimensional clean-slate approach are commonplace. Leaders who dismantle a company or operation *while* renovating it—demonstrating broad-dimensionality skills in the process—are rare indeed. Readers who have gone through their company being acquired by a larger entity will immediately comprehend the difference. During a typical acquisition, the small company is told that they are coveted because they have a new model, new competencies, and so on. Once acquired, however, the honeymoon phase gives way to stronger forces, such as the acquisition becoming measured by the institutional metrics of the mothership rather than the market-specific metrics of the new asset. In short: Managing the birthing of something new in a legacy sea is usually hindered by the legacy's processes and measurements.

- A longstanding culture's resistance to change creates a steady pressure manifested in attitudes about risk and change that drives decision making up the chain rather than in the direction where the change needs to be made. This reality of such resistance increases risk in an organization and elongates the time for change to occur.

- Resistance also places a premium on the engagement of leaders to understand the details of "how" to accomplish its goals. To reinforce this point, I was known to tell Avaya leaders about the time I was in Milan, Italy, for the close of an acquisition that ended shortly before Christmas Eve. My wife had not been thrilled that I'd be out of the country at that time. Following the end of the session, I was in a hurry to make my flight. But I also wanted to purchase a gift for my wife; a colleague recommended a nearby clothing store. In a rush I picked out a pink cashmere robe I was sure she'd like, paid for it, and continued on to the airport. I made it home as promised, and knew I'd made the right choice as I watched her face when she opened the gift. About a week later, my wife brought me our American Express statement, which contained a charge that could have purchased a small Italian car. I sheepishly admitted I hadn't looked at the price of the robe and had not calculated the exchange rate. Given how precious that garment is now, my wife wears it only once a year, on Christmas Eve, and has gotten a *lot* of mileage out of repeating that story of my poor judgment, year after year. It was a mistake that keeps on giving. In life as in business, details matter.

- Achieving an ever-improving customer loyalty and satisfaction while change is occurring internally is exceedingly difficult. At Avaya, it occurred largely by the measurement systems that maintained control and the alignment of the changes with items that were responsive to customer directions. Reaching an industry-leading NPS *during* the process was not something anyone could have predicted at the outset.

- The company developed a system to move the needle on financial metrics while achieving uncommon results. Few large high-tech companies will move EBITDA as a percent of revenue from 11% to 29%, or cause revenue/HC to nearly double to roughly $400K/HC, or EBITDA/HC to more than triple—reaching $100K. This is all the more astonishing, given that the results occurred post-recession with 28% less revenue than F2006.

While the numerical transformations above were far-reaching, they went well beyond what had been envisioned. For example, the original private equity business case for the company anticipated attainable productivity levels of EBITDA/revenue of 22% to 23% on higher revenues. By operating in the 26% to 29% range, the company was achieving five to seven cents more profit per revenue dollar than what had been considered likely, and eighteen cents more than its low point. Obviously, many companies can only dream of an EBITDA/revenue of 7% to 18%.

SYSTEMIC CHANGE

A successful transformation required looking at every process manifesting long cycle times, wide variance in the time it took to generate quotes, and poor customer satisfaction. With the introduction of (a) new streamlined processes, (b) systems that could absorb stochastic inputs and outputs, and (c) mechanisms to provide predictive insight, dramatic change took place. Automation with predictive

Systems matter for sustainable performance.

and integrative tools reinvented certain company functions, delivering benefits to customers and to Avaya's P&L statements.

Because of the Avaya experience, I now think of digital transformation as the reinvention of processes with automated, integrated, and predictive systems that ultimately reduce cycle times and interventions.

The flip side of this is teaching employees to think in terms of quantitative benefits. With automation—perhaps reducing by 50% the 150-member sales support pricing team who dealt with manual interventions and complexity—fixed costs might be reduced by $8M per year and variable cost might improve by another $4M to $8M per year. This resulted in as much as 250 to 500 basis points of EBITDA improvement year over year, a quantity relevant to employees in pursuit of bonus payout thresholds as well as something a Chief Financial Officer, Chief Restructuring Officer or Chief Executive Officer would highlight with investors. Thus, focusing a team on outcomes and the yield of their initiatives is essential.

MOTIVATING WITH OUTCOMES

This way of thinking allowed the leadership team to see serious opportunities for success. For instance, while reviewing headcount and financial reports, the team encountered a line item indicating that Avaya had roughly 40% of its headcount as Contact Center agents operating in more than 200 sites around the world. Over the course of a decade, as the company made acquisitions and for international language reasons, little cross-training had occurred, and there was essentially no self-service. An earlier international offshoring initiative had moved complexity overseas without appreciable improvement in the service. The result was an erosion of the quality of customer experience leading up to 2010.

We simply had to do better. Mike Runda, Senior Vice President for Client Services, led the initiative that contributed to a billion-dollar transformation. Mike and his team analyzed the three components of cost for voice-oriented Contact Centers: labor that could be roughly 85% or more of the cost structure, followed by telecommunications charges that could be 10% +/-, followed by operational software costs that could be roughly 5% of the total. Lowering the cost of labor was the place to focus, enabled by software.

The cost of labor led the company to focus on driving more customer resolution into self-service, which at the time of starting the transformation, was only around 4% of the total amount of contact with the Centers.

A serious and limiting factor at the beginning of the initiative was knowledge management. Avaya's older, internally developed system connected customers and agents with the right content approximately 88% of the time; the availability of the system operationally was about 90%. Both of these metrics are eight to ten percentage points beneath a best-in-class operation. Both metrics indicate that customers were waiting longer to obtain problem resolution: Minutes could and too often did stretch into hours.

From Mike's previous work at Oracle and other firms, he knew that system modernization could deliver correct knowledge management matches in seconds 96% to 98% of the time, and that the availability of the system operationally could reach 99.9%.

Thus, our first step was a focus on knowledge management. "Knowledge" in this case was a record in a database of customer interactions, status, etc.—who the buyers were, past purchases, bids or offers, loyalty points, last upgrade, etc. Avaya's home-grown application to manage this knowledge worked only 88% of the time—not good enough, especially if the goal was to develop self-service, cut costs, and increase customer satisfaction. We replaced our home-grown tool and bought an Oracle application that dramatically improved knowledge management and delivered the targeted system availability and speed required.

Next, we began a process for self-service—specifically, problem resolution via text. Adoption began, somewhat slowly at first, but accelerated with consistent growth. We then cross-trained agents across categories of products (rather than single products). Mike followed this by introducing a new policy (as noted earlier) requiring all agents to document their resolution to a problem within thirty minutes of having done so. This was a brilliant change since it ensured that customers, independent of what channel they came in on, would have at their disposal the most up-to-date knowledge and examples of resolution. Agents no longer spent unnecessary time on past problems. Before long, all problems became new problems. In fact, employee engagement grew 18% following this change—the biggest such shift in our collective memory.

A further step to improve adoption involved compiling customer calls in segments. Call-back assistance could be used for calls that were not time critical and for calls that asked how to gain access to voicemail if a password was forgotten. Now with call segmentation, the workforce could be level loaded and be more highly utilized.

Segmentation led to the addition of video calls where high-end enterprises wanted to be able to see our support staff. For these calls, Net Promoter Scores were in the mid- to high-50s while the bulk of the volume was tending toward text after eighteen months and NPS was in the 25 to 28 range, i.e. satisfactory. For calls that continued on voice, NPS was in the mid- to high-40s since empathy and context were more easily communicated.

After two years, more than 90% of inbound requests came in self-service mode with 62% resolved on the first attempt. The remainder were completed via voice or video with higher Net Promoter Scores. Overall, support service more than doubled the NPS. The number of agents was reduced by roughly 3,500. Over a four-year period, Avaya saved more than $1B, and customer satisfaction improved dramatically.

These outcomes have board-level significance as they impact the P&L as well as the balance sheet, and they are outcomes most companies in any industry can drive. This work had a profound impact on improving Avaya's business model and lengthening the runway. It is also a good example of transformation by dismantling the past in order to invent a new system.

QUALITY CONTROL

Another transformation effort occurred in Research & Development where we sought to cure several specific quality issues. (Some examples were mentioned in Chapter 10.) The key to achieving needle-moving outcomes was an inspection and compliance system put in place by Gary Barnett, Avaya's head of Product Development. The system included the concept of walls of fame and shame that called out teams and projects that were becoming predictable outliers. Conversation in the ranks became focused on getting good grades and avoiding the remediation calls. We learned just how powerful fear and peer pressure could be in driving employee performance. It was about a system that promoted individual awareness and accountability.

NEW CUSTOMER-ACQUISITION MODELS

While the business-to-consumer companies have provided frictionless online procurement for years, the business-to-business commercial dynamics still largely reside in a cul-de-sac of sales personnel, procurement organizations, and so on.

As of 2016, Avaya set its sights toward customers who wished to be served digitally. That is, they could browse the web, select a service from Avaya, try out the services, and pay for usage without any person-to-person engagement. Of course, this is not new in the consumer world, but at the time it was (and still is) far less prevalent in the B2B market.

Within six months of the new service, one customer had a run-rate of 67,000 voice minutes weekly, resulting in $10K per week in automatic payments to Avaya. Customer acquisition, the order, the subscription, and the payment were all now accomplished digitally. (See Figure 1 for the ascent of a new model for commerce.) I believe more of this will become the norm in the future—industry by industry, company by company, month by month.

Customer Success – Online Adoption

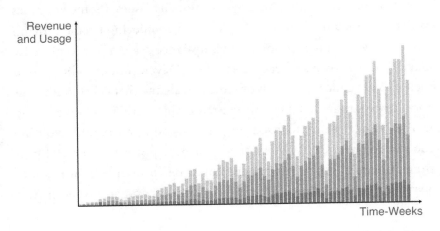

Chapter 11—Figure 1: A Touchless Cloud Adoption Model

This was a new business model for Avaya in which customers would not have to deal with an Avaya employee or partner representative, if that was their choice. Increasingly, sales representatives will become service consultants, as ordering and subscription take place without sales staff. New systems, predictive by nature, which automate out human complexity, make up the path to new business models and compelling business outcomes.

Digital transformation will be an ambidextrous journey, where automation and predictive analytics drive workflows that save large costs in legacy operations and will bring incremental improvements in Net Promoter Scores. In concert with these changes to the known operations of a company, new business models will be born that deliver new revenue growth and huge NPS gains.

The Customer Journey - Reality for Progress

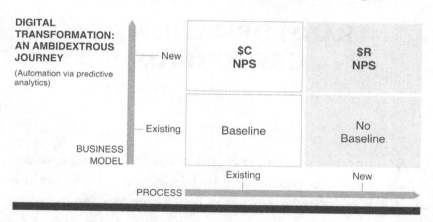

$C = Large cost savings from operational improvements
$R = Opportunity to drive large increases in revenue from new customers

Chapter 11—Figure 2: An Ambidextrous Journey

Figure 2 consolidates this concept of the improvement of legacy models to fund the growth and investment of new business models: In the legacy world, a known baseline exists; in the new process world, required for a new business model, there is no baseline. Dramatically making more efficient the current operational complexity can materially improve financials and remediate NPS. The investment in new processes for new business models drives significant growth frequently targeted at new customers and market segments, and it achieves dramatic gains in customer loyalty (NPS). In short, there is a dynamic complementarity in optimizing the present and driving future growth with new, all-digital paths.

~ 12 ~

TRANSFORMATION AT A CROSSROADS

Any reader who has purchased an older home and has under-taken a renovation project might initially envision patching holes, painting, replacing a light fixture here and there, and shoring up a sagging porch. Soon enough, it becomes obvious the flooring should be upgraded, rusted pipes need to be replaced, and a couple of kitchen appliances would emphatically announce "twenty-first century!" Then, once renovation is underway, the dimensionality of the project suddenly mushrooms to include new wallboard, a higher ceiling, code-compliant wiring, termite abatement, ad infinitum. Imagine doing all that during an unrelenting thunderstorm.

In the same vein, the prospect of tearing down and rebuilding Avaya was multidimensional, and the environment was not con-ducive. As one customer, George Sherman, a CIO in a New York bank and a customer advisor, remarked at the time, "You realize that the company died sometime in 2007-2008 and your team is seeking to resuscitate it, right?" Disquieting though his feedback was, I knew that George understood the rate at which the market and competitors were advancing and the depth and breadth of the legacy that required transformation.

What had been accomplished by the end of 2016 was impressive, by anyone's standard. The company had completely rebuilt its **solutions** (products, services), **competencies**, **culture** and **business model**. That said, two major hurdles remained before Avaya's transformation would be complete. Before we explore those, a brief recap of the achievements

> *Clear threads of revenue growth had been established with mix shifts underway.*

to date will help visualize the new company and set the stage for what followed in 2017:

Solutions

- Static, hardwired infrastructure to policy-driven dynamic applications
- Voice-only to omni channel

Competencies, Technology, and Products

- Hardware to software to virtualized software and containerized compute workloads
- Voice to voice, video, and data
- Circuits to packetized information with policy-based programmability
- Fixed voice communication to any channel mobile communication
- Proprietary technology to open standards

Culture

- From company-centric to customer-centric
- From telecom to computer to web
- From low productivity and manual to high productivity with automation

Business Model
- Corporate structure: from public to private to public
- From a product-dominated business model to a services-dominated business model
- From hardware to a software and services competency
- Sales: from one-time capital expense sales to recurring and subscription services including the cloud
- Scaling: from a people intensive low revenue per headcount and low EBITDA/HC model to high revenue and EBITDA/HC models (a software model-revenue per headcount of $350K to $400K and EBITDA/HC of roughly $100K/HC)
- From low operational excellence to superior operational excellence
- From low customer satisfaction to industry-leading NPS

In 2010, at the outset of the process whose results we've just recapped, Avaya's employee count was roughly 21,000. By the end of 2016 it was just shy of 10,000 (and of those, probably half were relatively new to the company). This dimension of the transformation was indeed uncommon, especially in the world of technology.

In addition to the shift in headcount productivity, two remaining structural transformations required advancement:

- The go-to-market structure, still largely a structure that resembled a legacy hardware company; and
- The balance sheet: By the end of F2016, net debt/EBITDA was roughly 6.1 (down from a peak of 7.1) and if other obligations were included such as pensions, the net effective debt/EBITDA was 8.6 (down from a peak of 10.1). Maturities were looming on some elements of the debt and costs were going to increase given the level of leverage.

As for the first hurdle, the go-to-market structure (more than 75% of the company's revenues) came from channel partners, despite the fact that in the new world of software and services, many partners were increasingly less prepared to deal with the software-and-service skills relevant to customers' needs. Both the business model and level of care were strained in the more hardware-oriented go-to-market structure that had not fully evolved for the market of 2016. Increasingly, customers were buying software direct from manufacturers, cloud providers, or a smaller number of more highly skilled partners.

The invention of new products, such as the cloud platform mentioned earlier, would eventually move the mix of revenue streams from the past to the future—i.e., from one-time purchases to recurring and subscription models paid out over time. Customer preference and the nature of new solutions would provide a natural evolution to a future-state mix and equilibrium of purchases. The business would therefore expand, because customers would exert a pull and as the change occurred, the company would continue to have the opportunity afforded by its business model to further develop according to whatever mix shift occurred.

With the go-to-market structure on its own path, the remaining hurdle was overt action required relative to the balance sheet. In a similarly anachronistic thread, the debt structure was a holdover from a pre-recession set of assumptions. Avaya had persisted with a capital structure that was still highly levered as summarized above, with roughly $6B of basic debt. With each successive amend and extend of prior debt tranches, newer and higher interest rates had brought more refinancing fees and the possibility loomed that debt service obligations could increase by 50% or more.

By May 2015, it was clear that the status quo debt structure and leverage had consumed the equity of the company. Avaya was rapidly running out of runway.

~ 13 ~

FINAL RESTRUCTURING HURDLE & DEBT REORGANIZATION

With the runway for debt maturities shortening, the Avaya board had undertaken an exhaustive process of looking at every conceivable option. Given the lack of a strategic buyer for the larger business—due primarily to the scope of debt and other obligations—that process (along with the advice of numerous consultants) eventually resulted in the sale of the networking business and the engagement of debt holders. Ultimately the board arrived at a point where a single path forward—Chapter 11 protection and debt reorganization—became the only viable option.

Even so, once filing is a *fait accompli*, the outcome drives a change in ownership of the assets to the lien holders/creditors, and the unknown duration of the process to exit a debt reorganization weighs heavily on everyone. In short: Filing is one thing; *accepting* this stage of a transformation takes some marination. Metaphorically, the process is not unlike a divorce—i.e., burdened by social stereotypes despite being necessary and relatively common.

On a personal level I found acceptance to evolve in stages. Shortly after Avaya had filed, at a board meeting of another company in February 2017 (shortly after Donald Trump's inauguration), a colleague turned to me and wryly observed that if someone files for Chapter 11 more than once, they might be considered to meet the minimum requirement for being elected president of the United States. I was aware that his comment was facetious, but at the same time I knew I was still coming to terms with accepting the magnitude of what was happening. Some of our consultants were of the mindset that "It's no big deal." But for most people, bankruptcy has a hugely negative connotation—it *is* a big deal! And not knowing how long the process would take only added to everyone's stress level.

While I knew it had to be done—and the sooner we got started, the better—I don't mind admitting that I didn't know how to manage people's expectations. So, I began to take a look at other companies' bankruptcy stories, thinking that they might reveal insights to help assuage the fears of Avaya's employees, customers, and other stakeholders. Some big-name companies had gotten through it (Kodak, Aspect) while others hadn't (Nortel). I started calling leaders who'd been through it to learn as much about their experience as I could.

> *Filing is one thing; accepting this stage of a transformation takes some marination.*

I also explored the subject of bankruptcies in history. What I learned is that many well-known and highly successful people in history have gone through personal or affiliated bankruptcy, including four earlier US presidents (Lincoln, Grant, McKinley, and Jefferson—all *prior to being elected!*); three other presidents liquidated assets to deal with debt. In most cases, debt was a difficult but necessary partner when unforeseen events (crop failures, failed business ventures, inherited obligations, et al.) occurred.

All of that reinforced the knowledge that debt brings risk to companies that are vulnerable to economic downturn. Yet prior to a downturn, the risk usually seems worth it: Debt is simply one part of the cost of doing business. Understanding that helps keep major debt reorganization in perspective—i.e., it is simply another piece of the puzzle in how to successfully advance a transformation.

I remember once having to think of a good way to clearly explain the debt reorg process at a major customer event, in a way that individuals not fiscally trained could understand. An analogy proved useful, based on a challenging medical issue occurring at that time in my family: One of our granddaughters had been born prematurely, necessitating a three-month stay in neonatal care; around the same time, her big sister, age two, was diagnosed with a faulty valve that was supposed to preclude backwash from the bladder into her kidney, which had caused repeated infections. Once the issues were identified, we consulted with medical experts, who proposed interventions and processes with which we weren't familiar, didn't know the duration of, and so on. Thereafter, the treatments evolved to where healing could begin and each girl was able to grow normally. As with the business, Avaya's issues had been diagnosed, we sought counsel from advisors, and once we had filed for Chapter 11, we believed that the "cure" would manifest over time to a successful conclusion. The true story I shared with them was something they could relate to. For the rest of that customer event, attendees focused their attention and questions on products and services, not the debt reorg.

Nothing is guaranteed, of course, in life or in business. An example of what can happen when debt encounters the unforeseen occurred in 2012. Monitor Group, a Cambridge consulting firm, had been co-founded by Harvard's esteemed and preeminent business consulting expert, Michael Porter. Porter was revered for his skills at strategic assessment through a critical examination and understanding of competitive forces. In spite of Porter's reputation and expertise, in 2008, in the throes of recession, Monitor's consulting work slowed dramatically, as their customer base deferred discretionary spending and focused on survival. There was significant debt: Monitor had borrowed more than $50M from the private equity firm Caltius Capital Management. Monitor's business model did not support their expense run rate: By September 2012 the company could not pay monthly rent and missed an interest payment to Caltius. Monitor filed for bankruptcy protection and was sold to Deloitte Consulting as part of a court-sponsored auction.

The so-what here is clear:

- Debt is inelastic and a difficult dance partner when the unforeseen is an adverse condition that impacts the business's top line.
- The recession of 2008-09 was a harsh reality to debt-laden assets.
- The difference between survival and the end of days translates to the strength of the business model, the reciprocal exchange of value between the company and customers, and operational excellence.
- A debt reorganization is a risk associated with debt albeit an enabler for companies that offer customer value and possess a strong business model.

The purpose of this chapter is not to belabor the details of the Chapter 11 process. Nonetheless, there are five crucial elements that a strong board and leadership team must stay focused on once the decision to file occurs:

GET OUT QUICKLY

Once you file, there must be clear intention to exit the process as rapidly as possible. The longer a company stays in the court-managed process, the less likely the company will emerge and the more likely it will liquidate. In this regard, prioritizing resources and removing roadblocks to the work that a myriad of advisors must accomplish is critical. Urgency drove Avaya to exit the process in eleven months. Given the size and complexity of the debt reorganization, that period was well within the recognized range for successfully emergent situations.

HOLD THE BUSINESS MODEL

The business model must be maintained, for if it is allowed to deteriorate too much, it becomes hard to size future debt-service expectations, thus prolonging the period while in Chapter 11 and increasing the downside risk associated with longer filing periods.

In technology companies, this can be a difficult mission as competitors will actively seek to move revenue away from a company in Chapter 11 to mitigate potential risk. Executing on this front in a technology company requires strong focus on customer service in concert with ongoing prudent productivity improvement actions that were par for the course at Avaya. Revenue and EBITDA did drop during this period, but the business model held relatively constant and actually improved with the sale of the networking business. This in turn enabled the company to accurately size future debt.

NURTURE CUSTOMERS

During Chapter 11, advocates within the customer base come under extreme pressure to reduce risk. Thus, it was imperative for Avaya's leadership team to regularly reach out to its customers. Since the duration of the process is not fully known by anyone, one can and should engage customers as Avaya did:

- Customers were regularly provided facts and insights on the process. We did not make commitments that we could not control.

- Customers were assured that they would see no change in (a) the way they were being serviced; (b) the high quality of software they were now using; and (c) product development and delivery timelines.

- Customers were given executive-level prioritization on high profile service installations or if issues were looming.

Through visits to hundreds of customers, the Avaya team faithfully executed the above, utilizing resources at headquarters as well as at regional facilities.

CAPITAL STRUCTURE SIZING AND RISK

As mentioned earlier, after much analysis, debt sizing often fits within a model where net debt/EBITDA ranges between 5 and 7. Keeping the net effective debt/EBITDA (with other obligations) to within the 5 to 7 range under downside scenarios increases the ability of a complicated asset to continuously delever.

That said, it's worth pointing out that a more complete perspective for complex assets could allow for the risk-adjusted consumption of cash under downside scenarios and the presence of legacy obligations, which could be considered a "net effective debt/EBITDA."

It may be useful to describe several sources of risk-adjusted cash consumption in adverse economic cycles:

1. Restructuring
   a. the costs of non-utilized assets (rents, long-term contracts);
   b. the high cost of exiting certain employees, such as unionized labor in Belgium, Germany, France, Italy, and others, where severance periods as high as twenty-two

to twenty-eight months equated to $250K to $500K per employee;

c. other fixed overheads.

2. Debt service
   a. increases in debt service as interest rates rise or risk rises;
   b. debt covenants that preclude a company from buying back debt at the publicly trade value, rather than at PAR value;
   c. refinancing costs.

3. Pension obligations that increase over time when interest rates drop or actuarial tables extend life expectancy and therefore require plan increases.

An obvious conclusion is that software and services businesses carry significantly less risk, especially if the workforce is not associated with pension costs or high-cost country workplaces.

Capital Structure Sizing - Risk Adjusted

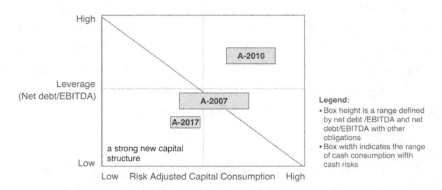

Chapter 13—Figure 1: Capital Structure Assessment

In Figure 1, Avaya existed from 2008 to 2017 with stated net debt/EBITDA ranging from 5.3 to 7.1, but adding other obligations this effective metric expanded to 8.6 to 10.1. The restructuring cost and escalating costs of other obligations occurred due to a world changed by the 2008 recession, an unforeseen risk.

By December 2017, Avaya emerged from a debt reorganization in the natural comfort of a lower net debt/EBITDA and a software and services company with lower risk, since the company had eliminated complexity and its inherent risks. Customers, employees, and owners all benefit from the new capital structure.

OUTCOMES MATTER

The exit from a Chapter 11 process takes shape when there is a confirmable, creditor-agreed plan of reorganization. At that point the process as well as the new owners exert a pull that enables a more predictable path to exit. In Avaya's case, the plan was agreed to in August 2017, with the emergence set for December 15, 2017. Announcing the agreement had a transformative effect, because we could inform interested parties that the go-forward balance sheet

Debt is inelastic and a difficult dance partner.

would evidence half the debt, and half the pension obligation; the company was to be traded publicly on the NYSE and a resulting increase of free cash flow of over $200M per year. The net debt/EBITDA would now be estimated in a range of 3 to 4, consistent with many public technology companies.

While 2017 was a difficult year operationally and the debt reorganization was a difficult experience for all involved, the experience achieved strong and enabling outcomes: Having completed the transformation of the debt structure, the company ended fiscal 2017 with revenues of $3.27B, an EBITDA/revenue of 26.6% (a company record), and a software and services mix of more than 78%. Recurring revenues topped 56% and the company was free cash flow positive during the fiscal year.

These results were made possible by the business model and operational excellence, atypical for a company transiting a debt reorganization process. A longer process, a weaker business model, a loss of customer engagement individually or in aggregate, could have steered Avaya to a non-sustainable outcome. The echoes of Nortel's liquidation, which had lurked in the background throughout Avaya's transformation, were finally and convincingly silenced.

~ 14 ~

A NEW RUNWAY & LESSONS LEARNED

Avaya emerged from debt reorganization through its transformation on multiple fronts:

- A telecom hardware company that navigated three business model changes (hardware to software; one-time to recurring revenue; service-centered solutions with products).
- A legacy company that drove transformational change to emerge with record financial metrics even as it was going through the debt reorganization process.
- An organization with a new business model featuring a superior go-forward strategy and capital structure.
- A company that achieved best-in-class Net Promoter Score through innovation and operational improvement even as the transformation process was underway. (Innovation was the quiet driver of superb loyalty scores.)

Creating value ultimately requires either a resuscitation of growth or the monetization of growth. Internal execution is highly desirable, but an equal component to that is mergers and acquisitions

103

which can assist, reposition, and bring crucial skills or intellectual property. Therefore, a balance sheet that enables M&A is a useful weapon for driving growth in a transformation. When possible, buy the future, not the past.

In terms of human capital, Avaya's emergence from its debt reorganization (versus the earlier path of liquidation not taken) meant:

- A future-oriented narrative with customers
- The completion of a change of ownership
- The maintenance of jobs for thousands of employees and contractors
- The protection of pensions to many thousands of former employees
- The continuation of products and services to hundreds of thousands of customers
- The continuation of products and services deployed by tens of thousands of partners whose employees depend on those products and services every day.

In short, the outcome was a victory for many people. It has been estimated that more than 250,000 people were better off for Avaya's emergence from its debt reorganization.

Looking back, and knowing what I know now, what are some things I would do differently if I had it to do over?

- Spend more time with those who are excited about transformation and building for the future.
- Act much sooner to let go of underperforming leaders.
- Spend more time teaching the team these truisms:
  o Runway is everything, and the CLIMB model optimizes its extension.
  o The impact of innovation on Net Promoter Score cannot be overstated.

- o A Value Creation Compass helps maximize allocation of resources.
- o Transformation requires acute focus on the "how"—not just the "what."
- Invest more time and effort exploring the opportunity (e.g., in 2011) to go out into the public-equity market at a presumably large discount, due to the enormous debt load. Instead, the owners wanted to wait, to put more history behind it. Hence, this option was not fully explored.

Beyond that, what are the key takeaways from Avaya's experience?

A CALL-TO-ARMS IS ESSENTIAL TO INAUGURATE SUBSTANTIAL CHANGE.

Once a crisis has been declared, assembling the right leadership and asserting initiatives to incubate the right biases is vital to setting and managing expectations. This is followed by metrics that capture the new business model to drive and build intensity around becoming the benchmark. The CLIMB model enables the management of expectations for the long haul. This approach then calls for a model for maximizing value and the allocation of resources—what became Avaya's Value Creation Compass.

LEADERSHIP MAKES ALL THE DIFFERENCE.

The leadership selection process establishes a signature and tone for delivering on expectations. Among the eight elements of hiring successful leaders outlined earlier, three stand out as key to ensuring a new leader's success during a transformation, based on Avaya's experience:

- Outstanding domain experience, having demonstrated best-in-class thought leadership in their area of expertise—whether in product management, sales, facilities, finance, et al.
- Detailed, relentless, daily inspection of process, progress, and results.
- Teamwork, especially cross-team coordination and support, along with the ability to motivate team members resistant to change.

SUSTAINABLE CHANGE REQUIRES SYSTEMIC CHANGE.

The greatest resistance to change is often internal. Be aware, be thoughtful, and use technology to systematically introduce change and new models. Creating sustainable change requires systems thinking. Outmoded systems must be disassembled; new systems must be predictive and integrative—establishing clear alignment of reported metrics that drive the daily rhythm and momentum of the transformation. Said another way, it is harder for an entrenched, entitled culture to defeat a system where success can be seen and measured.

> *Success is more likely determined by the "how" of change.*

TRANSFORMATION TAKES TIME.

When strategic directions languish, as when they've been built on the premise of a certain level of debt, it is usually the big assumptions that falter, such as an unforeseen recession, or a change in industry structure or competition.

THE BUSINESS MODEL MATTERS.

It extends the runway of a company. The movement of the business model from telecom hardware to software and services and initial movements to the cloud were profound at Avaya. Typically, legacy obligations during a transformation chew up margins and amplify the risk of execution. Fortunately, Avaya had sufficient cash reserves and a solid business model that allowed extension of the runway.

FINAL THOUGHTS

We live in a time when powerful technologies will continue to drive the disruption of virtually all tasks and activities, in every industry. Change will continue to require the invention of new business models for capturing commerce. Especially in the realm of communications, applications are absorbing infrastructure and the business model is increasingly about content and its connection to human- or machine-based outcomes. Digital transformation is essential for mobilization in an increasingly business-to-consumer commercial world.

Corporate transformation is primarily a board-level mission requiring structure, solid planning, courage, commitment, and the right talent to define the "how" to get the work accomplished. Underestimating the "how" is what leads companies to persist in the past long after competitors consume the future. Transformation must take place within the forward motion, metrics, and pace of an industry to avoid running out of runway due to economic cycles, competition, capital structure, business model, industry structure, or all of the above.

Runway is everything.

Ultimately, though, a successful transformation is about more than the board or CEO or leadership team. It's more than the strategies or models employed. It is, in the end, about the people who make it happen—every day, boots on the ground, applying their skills and experience in a common enterprise, even when the goal isn't always clear.

In the end, the time and scope of transformation matters, capital structure matters, and industry structure matters. These three factors define the runway, and as should be crystal clear by now, runway is everything.

At the end of its ten-year journey as a private company, Avaya emerged as an unlikely survivor against the odds, with a new runway that is secure and purposeful. Now, a company that traces its roots back 140 years to a small lab in Boston looks to a future as bright and impactful as its storied past. For those who lived Avaya's journey on a daily basis—who had faith and focus and contributed in ways that can never be fully chronicled—this is their story.

ACKNOWLEDGEMENTS

The Avaya story and the elements of an ever-expanding runway represents the work of many people. Reflecting back on the leaders who made the transformation of Avaya—and thus this story—possible, I feel a deep sense of admiration and gratitude.

First of all, the transformation of Avaya from a telecom hardware company to a software and services company required a sustained commitment by the private equity owners, Silver Lake and Texas Pacific Group (TPG) who took the company private in 2007. In particular, through 2017 Avaya had the good fortune to be served by John Marren and Greg Mondre, who led the board for TPG and Silver Lake, respectively. Charlie Giancarlo and Afshin Mohebbi knew the product categories and competition from personal experience. Mary Henry, Kiran Patel, Ron Rittenmeyer, and Gary Smith served with a broad range of investor, financial, and sales experience.

Several important board contributors who served the company after the go-private transition include Dave Roux, Avaya board chair and co-founder of Silver Lake Partners; Kevin Rollins, TPG advisor and former Dell president; Gene Frantz, former TPG partner now at Google. Nehal Raj, currently a TPG principal, was engaged with Avaya and the board for the majority of the transformation. It's worth noting that as boards deal with difficult decisions, the dynamics of a collection of individually bright people can sometimes be collectively underwhelming. The Avaya board members and process revealed a group of individuals willing to invest the requisite time, talent, and resources, and proved to be collectively compelling.

A number of the Avaya leadership team left a strong impact and transitioned to career-advancing roles beyond Avaya. These individuals include (but are not limited to) Mohammed Ali, Joel Hackney, and Pierre-Paul Allard.

The company's executive team all contributed in shaping the outcomes. Jim Chirico set up the systems for driving transformation and took the helm of Avaya in October 2017. His focus on execution served the company well and will continue to do so.

Amy Olli, Laurent Philonenko, and Dave Vellequette brought unparalleled professionalism as the company endured the stress of assessing strategic options and driving urgency through the debt reorganization process.

Gary Barnett, Jerry Glembocki, Marc Randall, and Mike Runda guided unprecedented progress in product quality, innovation, and customer care. Roger Gaston was central to the leadership development work.

John Sullivan, Avaya treasurer, was an incredible source of material for balance sheet related topics over time. Nidal Abou-Ltaif, Jim Geary, and Galib Karim emerged as superb sales leaders, maintaining an intense focus on customers and talent. Their professionalism shined throughout the transformation.

It is difficult to execute a transformation without the loyalty of customers and partners. Avaya leadership recognized this, and while there isn't space here to mention them all, without a doubt they deserve a huge Thank You. For Avaya leaders who listened to those customers and partners, there was no shortage of learning.

Throughout the years of transformation there was an opportunity to meet employees at all levels and in all regions of the world who cared, listened, and served with great insight, passion, and fearlessness. These individuals and teams will be well served in all they seek to accomplish.

* * *

As for the manuscript itself, I am indebted to a thoughtful and talented team of reviewers for their investment of time, quality of feedback, and variety of viewpoints. These reviewers include: Jake Chacko, Dave Kristoff, Katherine Kennedy Allen, Afshin Mohebbi, Corey Torrence, Mary Henry, Clare Libraro, and Pat Kennedy.

Similarly, a book like this requires particular skills to translate into accessible prose as it charts the experiences and perspective that deserve to be shared. George Mason's copyediting expertise and Clare Libraro's graphic talent were instrumental in producing this case study for the understanding and enjoyment of a wide variety of readers.

Finally, special thanks to my daughter Katherine who contributed as a researcher, intense critic, feedback loop, and collaborator on concepts as she compared the relevance of this case study to the more academic writings on organizational development in which she is immersed in her pursuit of a doctorate in that field. Her ability to find the time to assist in this enterprise while managing her other responsibilities was amazing and is deeply appreciated.

SOURCES

Grosvenor, Edwin S. and Wesson, Morgan (1997). *Alexander Graham Bell: The Life and Times of the Man Who Invented the Telephone*. New York: Harry Abrams.

Shulman, Seth (2009). *The Telephone Gambit: Chasing Alexander Graham Bell's Secret*. New York: W.W. Norton & Company.

Weinberg, John. "The Great Recession and its Aftermath," Federal Reserve Bank of Richmond, www.federalreservehistory.org (November 22, 2013).

Bureau of Labor Statistics. "The Recession of 2007-2009," www.bls.gov (February 2012).

Center on Budget and Policy Priorities. "Chart Book: The Legacy of the Great Recession" (November 7, 2017).

Amadeo, Kimberly. "2009 GDP Statistics, Growth and Updates by Quarter," www.thebalance.com (November 22, 2016).

MacDonald, Larry. "A Brief History of Nortel Networks," www.seekingalpha.com (November 22, 2016).

Reuters staff. "Timeline: The Key Dates in the History of Nortel," www.reuters.com (June 14, 2009).

McKinsey & Co. "How to Beat the Transformation Odds," Jacquemont, David; Maor, Dana; Reich, Angelika (2015). https://www.mckinsey.com/business-functions/organization/our-insights/how-to-beat-the-transformation-odds

The Economist. "Monitor's End" https://www.economist.com/blogs/schumpeter/2012/11/consulting

Denning, Steve. "What Killed Michael Porter's Monitor Group?" https://www.forbes.com/sites/stevedenning/2012/11/20/what-killed-michael-porters-monitor-group-the-one-force-that-really-matters/

Posen, Robert C. "The Underfunding of Corporate Pension Plans," The Brookings Institution (September 4, 2012). https://www.brookings.edu/opinions/the-underfunding-of-corporate-pension-plans/

BIOGRAPHY

Kevin J. Kennedy

Kevin J. Kennedy was previously the President and Chief Executive Officer of Avaya Inc., a global provider of fully-integrated, digital communications software and services. Kevin joined Avaya in 2009 and led one of the industry's strongest executive teams to create superior technology and help customers drive communication experiences.

Highly skilled at orchestrating innovation and change in communications and related industries, Kevin has over four decades of experience at companies including Cisco Systems, JDSU, Openwave Systems, and AT&T Bell Labs. Kevin's specialization is transforming companies through growth and company reinvention, tapping both organic innovation and mergers and acquisitions. During his career, Kevin has been instrumental in closing over 155 acquisitions and has double-digit asset divestitures.

Kevin currently serves as a member of the President's National Security Telecommunications Advisory Committee, a position he assumed under US President Barack Obama. In 1987, Kevin served as a Congressional Fellow to the US House of Representatives Committee on Science, Space and Technology. Kevin was honored by the School of Engineering at Rutgers University as their Alumnus of the Year and awarded an Alumni Medal of Excellence in 2006. He previously served on the Board of Regents at Loyola Marymount.

Kevin's board experience spans both public and private companies across numerous industries including enterprise software, semiconductors, semiconductor test and measurement, intellectual property, cloud infrastructure, real estate investment trust, and cancer research. Kevin has authored multiple patents and has published more than thirty papers on computational methods, data networking, and issues of technology management. He is the author of *Devil in the Details*, published in 2012, and a co-author of *Going the Distance: Why Some Companies Dominate and Others Fail*. Kevin holds a BS in Engineering from Lehigh University as well as MS and PhD degrees in engineering from Rutgers University where he served as an adjunct professor from 1982-1984. Kevin also holds a Distinguished Leader Executive Certificate from the University of Michigan Ross.

Kevin lives with his family in Silicon Valley, California, and can be reached at kjkenned690@gmail.com.

CPSIA information can be obtained
at www.ICGtesting.com
Printed in the USA
LVHW030430250220
648116LV00003B/508

9 781949 642179